ARGENTINE POLO PHRASE BOOK

AND WORDS

Revised edition published 2012 by Fast-Print Publishing of
Peterborough, England.

FastPrint Publishing

www.fast-print.net/store.php

Argentine Polo Phrase Book and Words

ISBN: 978-178035-421-7

A catalogue record for this book is available from the British Library

An environmentally friendly book printed and bound in England by
www.printondemand-worldwide.com

Mixed Sources
Product group from well-managed forests, and other controlled sources
www.fsc.org Cert no. TT-COC-002641
© 1996 Forest Stewardship Council
FSC

PEFC Certified
This product is from sustainably managed forests and controlled sources
www.pefc.org
PEFC
PEFC/16-33-415

This book is made entirely of chain-of-custody materials

R. Columba - A. Degrossi

ARGENTINE POLO PHRASE BOOK

AND WORDS

The essential reference for every player

Columba, R. - Degrossi, A.
Argentine polo phrase book and words
1a ed. - Buenos Aires.

Original ISBN 978-987-02-4279-6

1. Lexicografía - Terminología Deportiva. I. Título.
CDD 413.028

I have attempted to make the research and subsequent writing as accurate as possibly, but any mistakes and inaccuracies in this book stand as mine and only mine alone. RC

Any opinions and suggestions,
it will improve for next time.
paginascolumba@gmail.com

Drawings credit Francisco Pascual

e-mail: paginascolumba@gmail.com

I wish to thank H. Dupleich, J. Horswell, H. Pearl, J. Nicholls and M. Brett. I am warmly grateful for their help and comments, making me avoid gratuitous embarressment and making the book possible to read and understand.

Foreword

Here is the book everyone interested in horses and polo has been waiting for.

A collection of over 4000 horseman's terms in English and Spanish (Argentinian). The country most renowned for polo is Argentina, hence this book is based on Arg. Spanish pronounciation (a regional and small variation of spanish).

This book will help you to reach moments of true understanding in a different language.

It's a cultural guide for those moments when you really need to know How and When things are done.

This polo dictionary gets straight to the point in every situation, in the yard or in the field, for instance.

With drawings that generously complement the text and enable the reader quickly to identify the terms.

You will also find here other essentials, like numbers, dates, and basics phrases and words.

The main idea is to get you involved quickly in two way communication wherever comprehension might be a problem.

If your grasp of the language is limited, then for all those who visit the Argentine, Spain or other Spanish speaking countries then this is an essential travel item to take with you.

To be able to communicate with your friends, instructors and grooms and to find out more about your ponies, their ailments and preferences, then I cannot recommend this book more highly. It will also help you to make your staff from the Argentine feel more welcome and appreciated when they are away from their home country."

Nicholas J.A. Colquhoun-Denvers
Chairman
Hurlingham Polo Association

Chapters

Pronunciation

This book has been written in a system of phonetic pronunciation so it can be read as though it were English, bearing in mind the notes below:

An overwriten syllable, ***bold***, tells you to accent or stress that syllable.
Pronounce each syllable as if it formed part of an English word and you will be understood fairly well.

Vowels:

A as in English 'cat' and 'arm'
E as e in English 'bed'
I as ee in English 'see' but a little shorter
O as o in English 'hot' but a little longer
U as oo in English 'lou'

Consonants:

B bveh, C seh, CH tch-eh, D deh, F eh-feh, G heh, H ahtcheh, J ho-tah, K kah, L eh-le, LL eh-lyeh , M eh-meh, N eh-neh, P peh, Q koo, R eh-rreh, S eh-seh, T teh, V beh, W doh-bvleh bveh, X eh-kees, Y ee, Z seh-tah.

The following are the main differences with spanish spoken in latin america or Spain.

J sounds like a gutural H.

S and Z, always sound like english letter S

LL and Y are pronounced "dj" as in deluge, 'LLave' sounds djaveh.

Use of the word "you" in Argentina

If you know the people well or they are significantly younger, you can address them with the familiar "vos" (boss) for "you".

When speaking to a stranger or to an older person you don't know well, you should use the formal word "usted" (oostehd).

For more than one person, whether you know them well or not, use the plural "ustedes" (oostehd- ehs).

Background notes

It is hard to generalize about people's behaviour across so much and so varied social and physical terrain, but certain features do appear to be common.

The most obvious is courtesy and formality when people meet.

Argentina has a strong and obvious European connection and rather different history. The cattle ranches and farms (campos and estancias) produce the beef, wheat, corn and soya, which Arg. mainly exports, and the capital Buenos Aires is highly cosmopolitan.

Enormous wealth , displayed in grand houses, shoppings areas and luxury hotels and restaurants, contrast with poverty of the shanty towns (villas miseria) that surround every major city.

The contrast obviously produces social tensions that explode from time to time.

You will find that Argentinians will readily invite you into their homes .When you enter a room, you should shake their hand, and it is customary to kiss the cheek of girls and ladies, once. The visitor should follow the custom and say "please" (por favor) and "thank you" (gracias) more often than one might in English.

In part it is an excess of formality, in part a genuine acknowledgement of the other person.

Most local people you meet will act with generosity, it seems that the poorest people are usually the most generous.

If you are invited into someone's home and offered food and drink, it is rude to refuse, whether or not you feel they can afford it.

Generally, this courtesy does not extend to punctuality.

It is not the intention of this Polo Dictionary to be a complete phrase book for common travellers. However we include the most common words and phrases you always use just to make it easier, always in relation to the polo world.

1 | GROOM

Accommodation	vivienda	veevee-ehnda
Are you interested?	le interesa?	leh eentehre-sah?
Car	auto	aouto
Cash	efectivo	efek***tee***bo
Contract for xxxx	contrato por xxxx	kontrahto pohr xxxx
Months	meses	meh-sehs
Date of arrival	día de llegada	deea deh shegahdah
Date of departure	día de partida	deea deh pahr***tee***da
Day off	día libre	deea leebreh
Do you drive?	maneja usted?	mah-neha oosted?
Do you enjoy it?	le gusta ?	leh goos-tah?
Eu passport?	pasaporte europeo?	pahsa-porteh eh-oorop-eh-o?
Has nothing to do	no tiene nada que hacer	noh tee-ehneh nahda keh ahser
Have a good trip	buen viaje	bwen b***vee-a***he
Have experience?	tiene experiencia?	tee-ehneh ekspeh-ree-ehnseea?
How do you write it?	cómo se escribe?	kohmoh seh eskreebe?
How old are you?	qué edad tiene?	keh ehdad tee-ehne?
Listen to me	escúchame	eskootchameh
Married - single?	casado - soltero?	kahsado - sohl-tehro?
Name	nombre	***noh***mbreh
speak english? (Do you)	habla inglés?	ah-blah een-glehs?
Summer	verano	veh-rahno
Telephone	teléfono	te***leh***-fono
Truck / lorry	camión	kah***meeon***
Wage	salario	salah-reeo
Want to know how , when and where?(I)	quiero saber el cómo, cuándo y dónde?	kee-ehro sahvehr ehl ko-mo, kwahndo ee dondeh?
What work do you do?	que trabajo hace?	keh trahbaho ahseh?
Winter	invierno	een-bvee-ehrno
Work permit	permiso de trabajo	pehr***m-ee***so deh ***tra***hbaho
You will have xx horses	tendras xx caballos	tehn-drras xx kabashos

THE YARD

2 | YARD and STABLES

Accessories	accesorios	akseh-***so***hreeos
Accommodation	vivienda	veevee-ehnda
Bad traveller	viaja mal	vee-aha mahl
Bed	cama	***ka***ma
Body	cuerpo	kwerpo
Box	caja	***ka***h-ha
Broom (yard/wide)	escobillón	esko-bvee-shoohnn
Brush	cepillo	seh***pee***-sho
Bucket	balde	***ba***hldeh
Clipper	tuzadora	two-sah-door-ah
Clip (to)	tuzar	two-sahr
Comb (to)	peinar	peh-ee-nahr
Curry comb	rasqueta	ras***ke***htah
Disinfect	desinfectar	des-eenfektahr
Door	puerta	pwehr-tah
Drinking trough	bebedero	bveh-bveh-dehro
Drinking water	agua potable	ahgwa poh***ta***hvleh
Driving licence	licencia de conducir	leeszen-seeah deh kondooseer
Droppings	bosta	bohsta
Dung	bosta(!)	bohsta(!)
Farrier	herrero	eh-***rre***hro
Feed (to)	dar de comer	dar deh komer
Feed	alimento	ah-leemento
Feeding	alimentando	ah-leementan-do
Fence	empalizada	empahlee-sahda
Field	campo	kahmpo

MANGER

GROOMING SET

CLEANING SET

YARD AND STABLES

First aid kit	botiquín	bvotee***keen***
Fly	mosca	***mo***hska
Fly repellent	repelente	reh-pelenteh
Fork	horquilla	orh***kee***sha
Gate	tranquera	trahn-kera
Graze	pastar	past-ar
Grease (oil) the hooves	engrasar los vasos	ehngra-sar louhs vahsos
Groom	petisero	pety-***se***hro
Grooming	cuidado del caballo	kweedado dehl kabasho
Hand clipper	tuzadora de mano	too-sahdohra deh mano
Hard feed	balanceado	balan-zeado
Hay rack	pastera	pastehra
Hobbles	maneas	mah-***neh***-ahs
Hole punch	sacabocado	zaka-bohkado
Hoof	vaso	vahso
Hoof grease	grasa de vasos	grahsah deh vahsos
Hoof Tester	pinzas de vasos	***peen***zsas deh vahsos
Hoof-pick	limpia vasos	limp-eea vahsos
Horse fly	tábano	***tah***bahno
Horse walker	caminador	kahmee-nador
Horseshoe nail	clavos de herradura	klahbvos deh eh-rra***doo***-rah
Hose	manguera	mang-era
Lift the foot up	levantar la mano	leh-bvantahr lah mahno
Light	luz	loos

HAY NET

HOBBLES

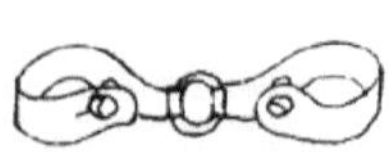

SHOE, STUD+NAIL

Lorry / truck/ horsebox	camión	kahm***eeon***
Lytes (electrolytes)	sales	sal-ess
Management	dirección	deereck***seeon***
Manger	comedero	koh-me***dero***
Menage (Arena)	picadero	peak-ahdehro
Muck out	hacer la cama	ah-sir lah kama
Muzzles	trompetas	trom-pettas
Nail	clavo	***klah***-bo
Nail up (to)	clavar	klah-***bar***
Paddock	potrero	poht-rehro
Partition	partición	part-ee***syon***
Pasture	pradera	prah-dehra
Pick out the hoof	limpiar los vasos	leempyar lohs vahsos
Pitch fork	horquilla	or***kee***sha
polo stud	taco	tako
Ramp	rampa	rampa
Rasp	escofina	esko-***fee***-nah
Remove the droppings	limpiar la bosta(!)	leempeeahr lah bohsta
Remove the shoe	sacar herraduras	sah-kar ehrra-doorahs
Room	cuarto	kwahr-to
Rug	manta	mahnta
salt lick	sal	sal
Scissors	tijeras	tee-***he***ras
Shade	sombra	***soh***mbrah
Shaving	viruta	vee-roo-tah

TWITCH

CLIPPER

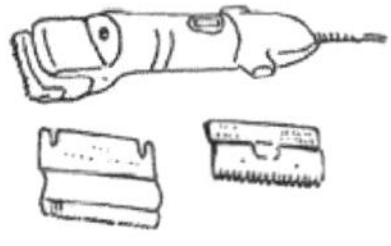

SADDLE RACK

YARD AND STABLES

Shelter	cobertizo	kober***tee***so
Shoe	herradura	eh-rra***doo***-ra
Shoe a horse (to)	herrar el caballo	ehrrahr l kabasho
Shoeing	herrando	eh-***rrahn-***do
Shovel	pala	pahla
Soap	jabón	ha-bohn
Sole	suela	swelah
Sponge	esponja	es***pohn***-ha
Stable	box	box
Stable bandage	venda de descanso	vehn***dah*** deh des***kah***nso
Stable / yard	caballeriza	kah-bah-she***ree***za
Stable-cloth	trapo	***tra***hpo
Straw	paja	***pah***-ha
Stud book	stud book	stud book
Stud fee	el costo de servicio	kohsto dell cerveeseeo
Sweat scraper	secador	sek-a- door
Tack room	monturero	montoo-***re***hro
Tail wrap/bandage	colera	kohl-era
To brush	cepillar	seh***peeh-shar***
To prick by farrier (will cause lame ness)	pinchar (produce cojera)	peen-tchar (proh***doo***se ko-hera)
Tools	herramientas	ehssa-mee-ehmtass
Trailer	trailer	trah-eeler
Transport	transporte	trahns***por***teh
Travel boots	botas de viaje	boht-ahs deh veeah-heh
Trim hooves (to)	desvasar	des-bvah-sahr

WHEEL BARROW

FENCE

TOOLS

Turn out (to)	soltar en el corral	zoltahr en l korrahl
Twitch	mordaza	mordazsa
Vices	vicios	***bee***-syos
Wash (to)	lavar	lavahr
Water	agua	agwa
Wheel-barrow	carretilla	kahrreteesha
Wipe dry (to)	secar	sekahr
Wormer	desparacitario	des-parahsit-ahryo

two very useful phrases

Tomorrow, start early ~ mañana, empezar más temprano ~ mahnyana, empeh-zar mahs temp-rrano.

You are sacked / fired! ~ estás despedido ! ~ ehstas despehdeedo !

FARRIER

SWEAT SCRAPER

HOLE PUNCH

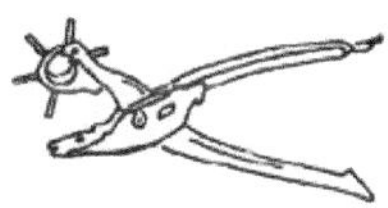

SHELTER

PADDOCK

TRAILER

3 | TACK

Accessories	accesorios	akseh-***soh***reeos
Analgesic cream	analgésico	ahnal-***he***hseeko
Arg. horseman	gaucho	***ga***ou-tcho
Back support	riñonera	rinyon-era
Ball	bocha	***bo***ht-cha
Bandages	vendas	venda-s
Barry gag	doble barra	dobleh bah-rrah
Bridle	cabezada	kah-bezada
Browband	frentera	fren-tehra
Buffalo hide	cuero de búfalo	kwero deh ***boo***-fah-lo
Coronet boots	protector de corona	protektohr deh korona
Coscojero	coscojero	kosko-hero
Curbchain	cadena de freno	kadehna deh frenoh
Drop noseband	cierra boca	sierra boka
Flap	solapa	so***la***pa
Girth	cincha	***seen***tcha
Groom	petisero	pety-sehro
Hackamore	jacamor	hackamore
Headcollar	bozal	bvo-sal
Hobbles	manea	mah-***neh***-ah
Lead rope	cabestro	ka***bes***tro
Martingale	bajador	baha-dor
Mouth piece	embocadura	embo-ka-doora
Muzzle	trompeta	trom-***pe***tta

GAG

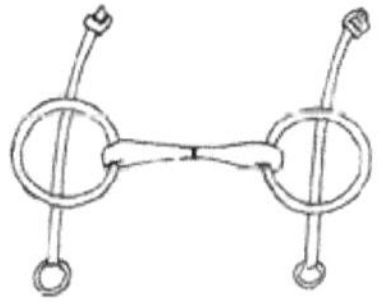

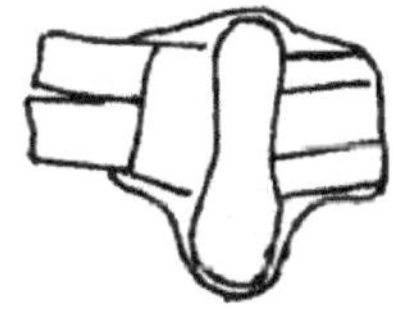

TENDON BOOTS

TAIL BANDAGE

TACK

Osteopath	masajista	mahsah-***gee***sta
Outdoor rug	manta de campo	manta deh kampo
Overreach boots / coronet boots	protector de corona	protektohr deh korona
Panel (saddle)	bastos	baastos
Pelham	pelam	peh-lam
Polo gag	levantador	leh-ban-tah-dor
Pommel	pomo	pomo
Raw hide	cuero crudo	kwero ***kroo***do
Reins	riendas	ree-ehndas
Rug	manta	mahnta
Running reins	riendillas	ree-ehndee-shas
Saddle cloth	matra	matra
Saddle	montura	mohn***too***rah
Saddle pad	goma espuma	goma espooma
Saddle tree	armazón	arma***thon***
Seat	asiento	ahsee-ento
Severe bit	freno severo	frehno seh-bero
Skid boots	pichiqueras	peetchikeras
Snaffle/ gag	filete	feel-ehte
Stable bandage	venda de descanso	vehndah deh deskahnso
Stirrups	estribos	estree-boos
Stirrup leathers	estriberas	estree-bveras
Stirrup lenght	largo de estriberas	largo deh las estree-***be***ras
Straps	tiras	teeras

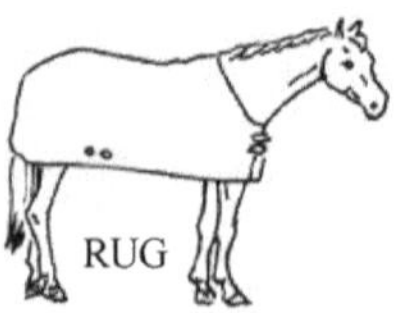

SADDLE CLOTH

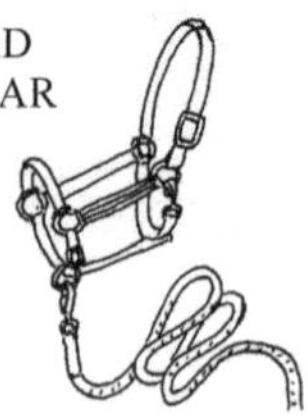
HEAD COLLAR

Summer rug	manta de verano	manta deh veh-rahno
Surcingle	sobrecincha	sobray***see***ntcha
Tack	equipo	eh***kee***po
Tack room	monturero	montoo***re***hro
Tacking up	ensillando	ens-see-shando
Tail/bandage	colera	kohl-ehra
Tape	cinta	seentah
Tendon boots	tendoneras	tehn-don-ehras
Tighten/ undo the girth	ajusta/ afloja la cincha	ahoosta/ a-floha la ***seen***tcha
Untacking	desensillando	deh-zen-seeshando

BRIDLE

GIRTH
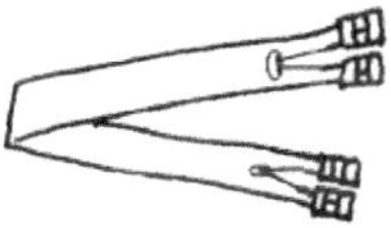

COSCOJERO with CURB CHAIN

BELL / CORONET BOOTS
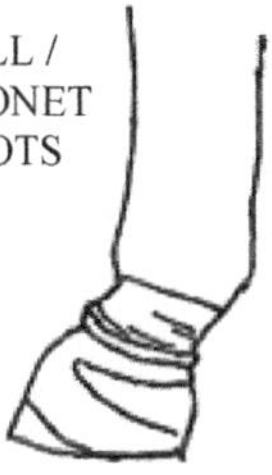

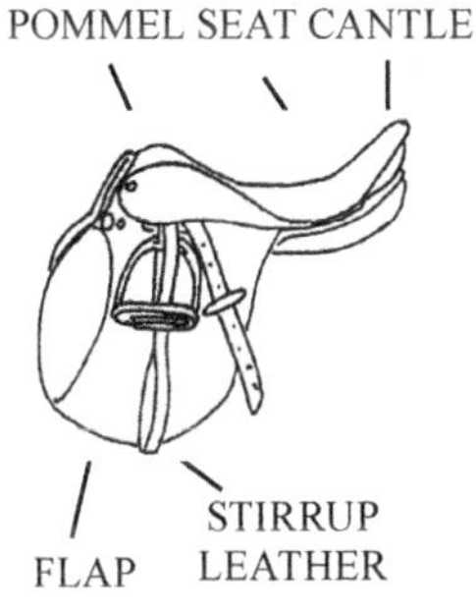

HACKAMORE BIT
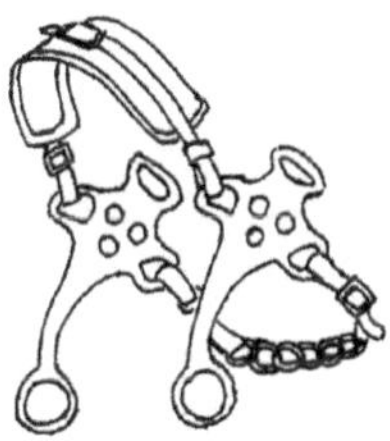

4 | RIDER'S EQUIPMET

Rider's Equipment	equipo	ehkeepo
Analgesic cream	analgésico	ahnal-***heh***seeko
Arg. Horseman	gaucho	***ga***ou-tcho
Back support	riñonera	rinyon-era
Ball	bocha	***bo***ht-tcha
Blue book	libro de reglas	leebro deh rehglass
Boot jack	sacabotas	saka bvo-tas
Boots	botas	bvo-tas
Chaps	chaparreras	tchapa-***rre***hras
Dictionary	diccionario	deekseeo-***na***rio
Donkey	burro	***boo***-rro
Faceguard	protector de cara	protek***tor*** deh kahra
Girlfriend	novia	no-beeah
Gloves	guantes	gwantehs
Goggles	antiparras	antee-***pa***rras
Half chaps	polainas	paul-ah-eenas
Horse (pony)	caballo	kabasho
Knee pads	rodilleras	rodee-sherahs
Mallet / stick	taco	tako
Masseur	masajista	mah-sa-heesta
Money	plata	pla-tah
Polo helmet	casco de polo	kasko deh polo
Spurs	espuelas	espwelas
Vaseline	vaselina	bvaseh-leena
Whip	fusta	foosta
Whites	blancos	blahnkos
Wrist support	muñequera	moonyeh-kera

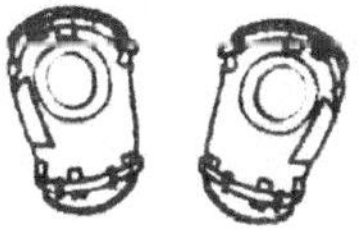

KNEE PADS

SPURS

TEAM SHIRTS

5 | TRAINING

Aids	ayudas	ah-shoodas
Arena	arena	arena
Bad	mal	mahl
Balance	balance	bah***lan***seh
Beginners	debutantes	deh-boo-***tahn***tehs
Behaviour	comportamiento	komportahmyento
Behavioural problems	problemas de comportamiento	provlemhas deh komportahmyento
Bitting	mordedor	mord-ehdoor
Bolting	desbocarse	dess-bo-karseh
Broken up (horse)	domado	dohmado
Buck	corcovear	korko-veh-ar
Canter / gallop	galope	gah***lo***hpeh
Change of direction	cambiar dirección	kambeear deerehk***seeon***
Change leg in the air	cambia las manos en el aire	kambya las manos ehn el ah- ee-reh
Change legs	cambiar de manos	kambeear deh mahnos
Coach	D. T.	deh-teh / coach
Cold back	lomo duro	lomo dooh-ro
Collect up (to)	reunir	reh-oo-neer
Collecting	colectar	kohl-ektahr
Condition	condición	kon-dee***syon***
Correct horse	caballo correcto	kabasho ko***rre***kto
Defects	defectos	dehfektos
Dismount (to)	desmontar	dehs-mohn-tahr

BEHIND THE GIRTH

AT THE GIRTH

TRAINING

Doesn't stop	no para	no pahra
Dry mouth	boca seca	boka sehka
Earlier	más temprano	mas temp-prano
Early training	entrenamiento temprano	ehntreh-nameeento temprahno
Energy	energía	ehner-***he***-ah
Excellent	excelente	exellenteh
Exercise (to lead)	varear	varayahr
Exercise in the morning...(to)	varear a la mañana...	varayahr ah lah mahn-eeanah
Exercise more minutes	ejercitar más minutos	eh-heseetahr mas mee-nootos
Exercise track	pista de vareo	peesta deh vareh-o
Experienced	experimentado	ekspehreementado
Fall (to)	caer	ka-ehr
Fall (a)	caída	kah-**ee**dah
Fast	rápido	***ra***peedo
Fat	gordo	gourdo
Figure 8	8 (ocho)	otcho
Fit	entrenado	entrehnado
Foot	pie	pee-eh
Give the reins	dar las riendas	dar las ree-ehndas
Good manners	buenos modales	bwenos modal-es
Grab	agarrar	ah-gahr-rrar
Green	verde	***beh***rdeh
Half seat	medio asiento	meh-deeo ah-see-ehnto
Hard ground	piso duro	peeso doo-ro

REARING

RIDING OFF

Hard mouth	boca dura	boka doo-rah
Heavy	pesado	peh-sahdo
Heavy hands	manos pesadas	mahnos peh-***sa***das
Heel down	talón abajo	talohn ah-baho
Hold the reins	tener las riendas	teh-ner las ree-ehndas
Horse action	acción del caballo	aksyon del kabasho
Horse walker	caminador	kahmee-nador
Impulse	impulso	eem***pool***so
Impulsion	impulsión	eempool***seeon***
Instructor	instructor	eens-trook-tohr
Kick (to)	patear	pate-ar
Later	más tarde	mas ***tar***-deh
Leading	de tiro	deh tee-ro
Lean on the bit	apoya en el freno	ahpo-sha en el freh-no
Leg	pierna	pee-ehrna
Light canter	galope liviano	gah***lo***-peh lee-bano
Loosen the reins	dar las riendas	dahr las ree-ehndas
lunging	a la soga	ah la zohga
Make a pony (to)	hacer un caballo	ahcehr oon kabasho
Mount (to)	montar	mohn-tahr
Mouth	boca	boka
Normal breathing	respiración normal	res-pee-rah***seeon*** noormahl
On the bit	afirmado	apheer-mahdo
On the left leg	zurdo	szoo-rdo

LUNGING

TRAINING

Outdoor school	picadero	peekadayro
Pipe opener	dar aire	dar ah-ee-reh
Polo helmet	casco de polo	kasko deh polo
Position	posición	pohs-see-***seeon***
Practice	práctica	***pra***kteeka
Rear up	encabritarse	enka-bree-tahrseh
Rearing	pararse de manos	pa***rar***seh deh mah-nos
Recovery	recuperación	rekoopeh-rah***seeon***
Rein back (to)	recular	rehkoo-lahr
Relaxed	relajado	rehla-hado
Rest period	período de descanso	peh-ree-oodo deh dehskanso
Restricted movement	movimientos restringidos	mobeemyentos restreen-he-dos
Ride bareback (to)	montar en pelo	montahr en peh-lo
Riding	cabalgar / equitación	kahbalgahr / aykeetah***seeon***
Riding lesson	Leccion de equitacion	lek***seeon*** deh aykeetah***seeon***
Satisfactory	satisfactorio	sateesfactoryo
School (to)	dar escuela	dar eskwehla
Shooling in a circle	dar círculos	dar ***seer***koolos
Shorten the reins	acortar las riendas	akortahr las ree - ehndas
Slow	despacio	des-***pah***seeo
Soft mouth	boca blanda	boka blanda
Soft ground	piso blando	peeso blando

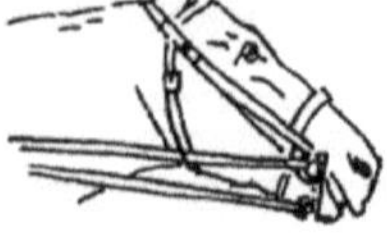

ON THE BIT

FALL

Start	comienzo	komee-enso
Stick and ball (to)	taquear	ta-keh-ar
Stop well (to)	para bien	pah-rah bee-ehn
Stretch the neck	estirar el cogote	estee-rahr el kogoteh
Thin / skinny	flaco	flako
Throw the rider (to)	tirar al jinete	teerahr al hee***ne***teh
To land	aterrizar	ah-teh-ree-tsar
Tongue over the bit	pasa la lengua	pah-sa la lehngwa
Track	pista	***pee***sta
Training	entrenamiento	ehn-treh-nameeento
Tripping	tropezarse	trope***sar***seh
Trot (to)	trotar	trotahr
Turns badly	dobla mal	dohblah mal
Unbroken	potro	pohtro
Unfit	desentrenado	dehs-entrenado
Unpleasant	desagradable	dehs-agradah-bleh
Very good	muy bien	moo-ee bvee-ehn
Vices	vicios	***bee***-syos
Walk (to)	caminar	kahmeenar
Warm up	precalentamiento	preh-kahl-ehntamee-ehnto
Wind sucker	tragador de aire	trahgahdoor deh ***ah***-ee-reh
Wooden horse	caballo de madera	kabasho deh mah***de***hra

LEADING

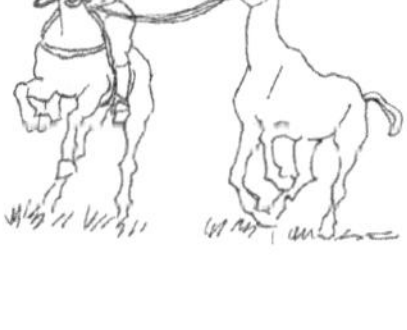

6 | MATCH

Accidents	accidentes	aksee-dentehs
Aggressive	agresivo	ahgrehseebo
Back !	back!	back!
Back! (shot)	back (tiro de)	back
Ball	bocha	***bo***ht-tcha
Ball shy	aparta de la bocha	ahpartah deh la botcha
Behind	atrás	ah-trahs
Best player	mejor jugador	meh-hor hoogadohr
Best pony	mejor caballo / yegua	meh-hor kabasho/ shegwa
Bet	apuesta	apoo-ehsta
Boards	tablas	tabl-ahss
Captain	capitán	kapitan
Centre!	centro!	zentro
Change (to)	cambiar	kambeear
Chukka	chuker	tcha-kehr
Close	cerca	sehrka
Coach	D.T.	coach/ deh-teh
Come back!	volvé!	ball-beh !
Cool down (to)	enfriar	n-freeahr
Crossing the line	cruzando la linea	kroo-sahndo la leeneea
Cup	copa	koppa
Danger	peligro	peh-***lee***gro

MATCH

Dirty player	jugador sucio	hoogah-door ***soo***seeo
Entry fee	costo matrícula	ma***tree***-kwla
Fairplay	juego limpio	hoo-ego ***lee***mpeeo
Fall (to)	caer	ka-ehr
Far	lejos	lehos
Field / ground	cancha	kancha
Fixed game	partido arreglado	pahr***tee***do ahrreglahdo
Foul	foul	foul
Free hit	tiro libre	teero ***lee***-bvreh
Front	frente	frehnteh
Game	juego	hoo-ego
Go!	anda!	ahnda !
Go back (to)	bajar	vah-har
Go up (to)	subir	soobeer
Goal post	arco	ahrko
Half chukka	medio chukker	meh-deeo tcha-kehr
Handicap	handicap	handicap
Hard ground	piso duro	peeso doo-ro
Here	acá	a-kah
Hit (to)	pegar	peh-gar
Hit it!	pegale!	peh-gal-eh !
Hook (to)	trabar el taco	trahbar l tahko
Hook it!	trabalo!	trahbalo !
Hose down the horse (to)	bañar el caballo	bahnyar l kabasho

TROPHY

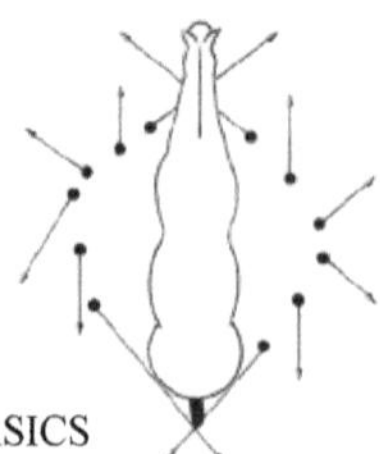

BASICS SHOTS

PLAIT TAIL(to)

Inside	adentro	ahdehntro
Learn to play polo	aprender a jugar al polo	ahprendehr a hoogahr al polo
Leave it!	dejala!	deh-hala!
Line of ball	lÍnea de la bocha	leenya deh la botcha
Line out	salida afuera	sal-eedah ahfwerah
Loser	perdedor	pehr-deh-dor
Mallet!	taco!	tako!
Match	partido	pahr***tee***do
Medium and high Goal	mediano y alto handicap	meh***dee***ano / ahlto handicap
Members	miembros	mee-embrross
Mine!	mía!	meea !!!
Nearside backhand	back de reves	back deh reh-bves
Nearside forehand	revés	reh-bves
Neckshot	cogote	kogoteh
Offside backhand	back	back
Offside forehand	por derecho	por dehretcho
Open !	abierto!	ahbee-ehrto !
Out	afuera	ah-fooehra
Out of bounds - off the field	fuera de cancha	fwera deh la kantcha
Over here	hacia aquí!	ah-seea ahkee!
Penalty	penal	pehnal
Penalty from the spot	penal del lugar	pehnal dehl lougahr
Plait tail (to)	trenzar cola	tren-zsar kola
Play it!	jugala!	hoogahlah!
Player	jugador	hoo-gah-door
Polo pony	caballo de polo	kabasho deh polo
Ponylines	palenques	pahl-n-kes
Position	posición	pohs-see-***seeon***

MATCH

Preparation	preparación	preh-parah-seeon
Referee	referi	reh-feh-ree
Ride him off!	sacalo!	sakahlo!
Ride off (to)	tomar	to-mahr- lo
Riding	cabalgar	kahbalgahr / aykeetah***seeon***
Right of way	derecho de paso	deh-rehtcho deh pahso
Rules	reglas	rehglas
Score	gol	gol
Shirt	remera	reh-mehras
Side	costado	cost-ahdo
Stop!	frena!	frehna!!
Tactics	tácticas	***tak***teeekas
Tail!	cola!	kola!
Take it! (ball)	tomala!	to-mah-la
Take the man	tomar al hombre	to-mahr al ohmbreh
Turn it!	redondilla!	reh-dondeesha!

PHRASES THAT MAY HELP

Give me the mallet....	dame el taco...	***dah***-meh ehl tako...
I play first / last	juego primero / último...	hoo-ego pree-***meh***-ro / oolt-eemoh...
I play tomorrow	juego mañana	hoo-ego mahnyana
The list of ponies is...	la lista de caballos es...	lah ***lee***stah deh kabashos s...
Mare xxx to the middle	yegua xxx al medio	shegwa xxx al mehdeeo
I play today...	hoy juego..	oi hoo-ego ...
The field is good	la cancha esta buena	lah kan-tcha stah bwena
How far is it to...?	qué tan lejos es...?	keh tan leh-hoos s ...?
Bank holiday	día feriado	deea feh-reea-do
Look out!	cuidado!	kwee-***da***do!
How much is it?	cuánto vale?	k***wa***nto bvaleh?

Team	equipo	eh***kee***po
There	allá	asha
Throw in	salida	sah***lee***da
Time out	tiempo fuera	tyempo foo-ehra
To me!	a mí!	ah mee!
Tournament	torneo	tor-neh-oh
Trophy	trofeo	tro-feh-o
Truck	camión	kahm***eeon***
Turn!	dobla!	dohblah !
Umpire	umpire	umpire
Umpire pony	caballo de referi	kabasho deh referi
Very bad player	choto	tchoto
Warm up	precalentar	preh-kalentar
Whistle	silbato	seal-bato
Winner	ganador	gahnador
Yards	yardas	tshardas
Your line!	tu línea!	too leeneea
Yours!	tuya!	tooscha!

MORE HELPFUL PHRASES

This mare is very bad	la yegua es muy mala	lah shegwa ehs mwee mahla
This mare is very good	la yegua es muy buena	lah shegwa ehs mwee bwena
The"pro" is asking too much	el "pro" pide mucho	ehl "pro" pee-deh ***moo***tcho
The saddle is loose	la montura esta floja	lah mohn***too***rah stah phloha
Tighten / loosen the girth	ajusta / afloja la cincha	ah-hoosta / ah-floha lah ***seen***tcha
Who won?	quién ganó?	kee-ehn gahno?
We have polo	tenemos polo	tehnehmos polo
You are sacked / fired!	estás despedido	ehstas despeh-deedo
Raining	lloviendo	shoo-bvee-ehndo

7 | VETERINARY PROBLEMS

English	Spanish	Pronunciation
Abcess in the hoof	abceso en el vaso	mach-oo-kon
Abort	abortar	ahbvourtahr
Abortion	aborto	ahbvourto
Accidents	accidentes	aksee-dentehs
Aggressive	agresivo	ahgreh***see***bo
Anaemia	anemia	ah-nehmeea
Anaesthesia	anestesia	ah-nes-***te***hsya
Antifungal	antihongos	anteeongos
Antiseptics	antisépticos	anteesepteekos
Artificial insemination	inseminación artificial	een-sehmeenah-***syon*** artee-fee-seeahl
Back pain	dolor en la espalda	dolohr n lah s-paldah
Bandages	vendajes	ven***da***-hes
Barren mare	yegua vacia	shegwa vahseea
Bee	abeja	ah***be***ha
Behaviour	comportamiento	komportahmyento
Behavioural problems	problemas de comportamiento	probvlehmas deh komportahmyento
Bite	mordedura	mor-deh-duhra
Blade	hoja	oh-ha
Bleed (to)	sangrar	sahn-grahr
Bleeding	sangrando	sahn-grahn-do
Blister	ampolla	ampo-sha
Blistering	cáustico	***cow***-steeko
Blood	sangre	sahn-greh

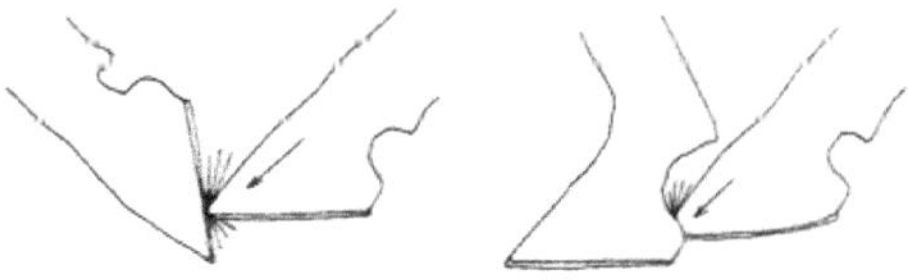

FORGING OVERREACH

VETERINARY PROBLEMS

English	Spanish	Pronunciation
Bone spavin inflamation	garrón inflamado	gah-rrohn eenflahmado
Broken	roto	rroto
Bruise	moretón / machucón	morayton / machoo-kon
Burns	quemaduras	kehmaduhra
Bute (phenylbutazone)	bute	bute
Changing the teeth	cambio de dientes (dentición)	kambeeo deh dee-ehntehs
Chest	pecho	petcho
Clean	limpio	***lee***mpeeo
Cold back	lomo duro	lomo dooh-ro
Cholic	cólico	***kohl***-leeko
Condition	condición	kon-dee***syon***
Conformation	conformación	konfor-mah-***syon***
Contagious disease	enfermedad contagiosa	ehnfermedad konta-heeosa
Cool down (to)	enfriar	n-free-ahr
Corn	cayo	kasho
Cotton-wool	algodón	algoodoon
Cough	tos	tos
Coughing	tosiendo	tosee-ehndo
Cracked heels	talones agrietados	tahlonehs agreeeh-***ta***hdos
Cracked hoof	rajaduras en los vasos	rahadowra en los vahsos
Cream	crema	krema
Cut	cortadura	korta-duhra
Debility	debilidad	dehbeeleedad
Defects	defectos	dehfektos

Diarrhoea	diarrea	dee-ah***rrea***
Diseases	enfermedades	ehnfermedah-des
Disinfect (to)	desinfectar	des-eenfektahr
Distortion	dislocar	dees-lo-***kahr***
Dizzy	mareado	mareh-addo
Dorsal vertebrae	vértebras dorsales	***vehr***-teh-brass door***sa***hlehs
Dressing	apósito	***apo***seeto
Energy	energía	ehner-he-ah
Equine influenza	gripe equina	***gree***-peh
Examination	examinación	eksa-meenah***seeon***
Fall (to)	caer	ka-ehr
Fall	caída	ka - ee - dah
Fat	gordo	gourdo
Fertilization	fertilización	fertee-leezsah***seeon***
Fever	fiebre	fee-eh-breh
Finadyne (flunixin Meglumine)	finadine	fee-nahdin
First aid kit	botiquín	bvoteekeen
Flexion test	prueba de flexion	prwebah deh flek***syon***
Foaling (its)	pariendo	pahree-ehndo
Foaling (adj.)	parto	pahr-tto
Fracture	fractura	fraktwra
Geld (to)	castrar	kastrar
Girth sores	sobaqueada	zsoba-keh-ada
Has it got a temperature?	tiene temperatura?	tee-ehneh tempehra-too-ra

WORMS

VETERINARY PROBLEMS

Have you got anything for...?	tiene usted algo para...?	tee-ehneh oosted ahlgo pahra...?
Healing	curando	kooh***ra***ndo
Hoof tester	pinzas de vasos	peenzsas deh vahsos
Horse fly	tábano	***tah***bano
Hose leg	manguerear	man-gheh-reh-r
How is?	cómo esta?	komo ehsta?
Ice	hielo	ee-ehlo
Infection	Infección	eenfek***syon***
Infectious anaemia	anemia	***ahne***meea
Inflammation	inflamación	eenflahmah***seeon***
Inflammation of a Joint/arthritis	inflamación de articulación	eenflahmah***seeon*** deh arteekoolah***seeon***
Influenza - cold (flu)	gripe, enfriamiento	greepeh / ehn-freeahmiento
In-foal mare	yegua preñada	shegwa prehneeada
Injection	inyección	eenjeck***syon***
Injuries	heridas	ehreedas
Intramuscular	intramuscular	inntramooskoo***lahr***
Intravenous	intravenosa	inntrahbvenosa
It hurts here	duele aqui	dweleh akee
Joints	articulaciones	rteekoolahseeonehs
Kidney	riñón	reenyon
Laminitis	laminitis	lah-mee-nee-tees
Lice	piojo	peeo-ho

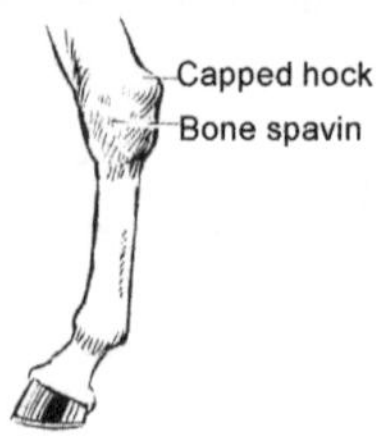

Ligament (suspensory)	ligamento (suspensorio)	leega***mehn***to (soos-pen-***so***ryo)
Ligaments	ligamentos	leega***mehn***tos
Liquid paraffin	parafina líquida	parahfeenah ***lee***keeda
Mare in foal	yegua preñada	shegwa prehnyada
Masseur/osteopath	masajista	mah-sa-***hees***ta
Masssage	masaje	ma***ssa***heh
Medicines	medicinas	mehdee***see***nas
Mud fever	infección cutánea	eenfek***syon*** koo***tah***nya
Muscle atrophy	atrofia muscular	ah-trofya mooskoo***lahr***
Muscle strain	desgarro muscular	des-***ga***hrro mooskoo***lahr***
Navicular disease	enfermedad navicular	pro-bvlehma navee-koo***lahr***
Normal respiration	respiración normal	res-pee-rah***seeon*** noormahl
Open wound	herida abierta	ehreedah ahbee-eh-rrta
Organs	órganos	***oo***rga-nos
Pain	dolor	doh***lohr***
Pain in the leg	dolor en la pierna	doh***lohr*** ehn la pee-ehrna
Parasites / Worms	parásitos	pa***ra***hseetos
pin firing	puntas de fuego	pwntas deh fwehgo
Pneumonia	pulmonia	poolmo***nee***ah
Poultice	compresa	kompressa

Pregnant	preñada	prehnyada
Pulled muscle	tirón (muscular)	teerohn mooskoo-***lahr***
Pulse (bits)	pulso	poolso
Pulse rate (bit rate)	pulsación	poolsa-***syon***
Pus	pus	poos
Quarantine	cuarentena	kwaren***teh***na
Rasp (to)	limar	leemahr
Recovery	recuperación	rehkoopeh-rah***seeon***
Red worms	estrongilos	es***tron***-heelos
Respiration	respiración	respeerah***seeon***
Rest period	período de descanso	peh-***ree***-oodo deh dehskanso
Restricted movement	movimientos restringidos	mobeemyentos restreen-he-dos
Raise the foot (to)	levantar la mano	lehbvantahr lah mano
Scissors	tijeras	tee-***he***ras
Skeleton	esqueleto	s-keleto
Spasm	espasmo	s-pasm-o
Splint	sobrehueso	sobrehgweso
Sprained tendons	tendones inflamados	tehn - ***don*** - s eenfla-mahdos
Stable	box	box
Stable bandage	venda de descanso	vehndah deh deskahnso
Sting	picadura	peekadoora
Stomach	estómago	es***to***-mahgo
Strain	desgarro	desgahrro
Strangles	paperas	pah-peras
Suffering from	parasitosis	parahseetosis
Surgery	cirugía	seer-oouheea
Sweat (to)	sudar	soodahr
Swelling	inflamación	eenflamahsyon

Swollen tendons	tendones inflamados	tehn-***don***-s eenfla - mahdos
Syringe	jeringa	hereengah
Takes good care of	cuida muy bien	kweeda mwee beeehn
Tape worms	tenias	tehneeas
Teaser	celo	sehlo
Tendon sheath	vaina de tendón	bah-ee-nah deh tehn-don
Temperature (normal 102 °F)	temperatura (normal 37.5-38 °C)	temperah-toora noor-mal 37.5/ 38°C
Tetanus	tétano	tehtano
Thermometer	termómetro	termohmetro
Thin	flaco	flako
Thread worms	oxiuros	ohkseewroos
Thrush (in hoof)	hormiguero	or-mee-ggero
To be in season	celo	sehlo
To be lame	cojear / aflojar	ko-heh-ahr / a-flo-har
Topical	superficial	superfee***syal***
Tripping	tropezarse	tropesarseh
Twitch	mordaza	mor***da***zsa
Vaccination	vacunación	bvakoonah***seeon***
Vaccine	vacuna	bva***koo***na
Vaseline	vaselina	bvaseh-***lee***na
Vet	veterinario	beh- teh-ree-***na***ryo
Vices	vicios	***bee***-syos

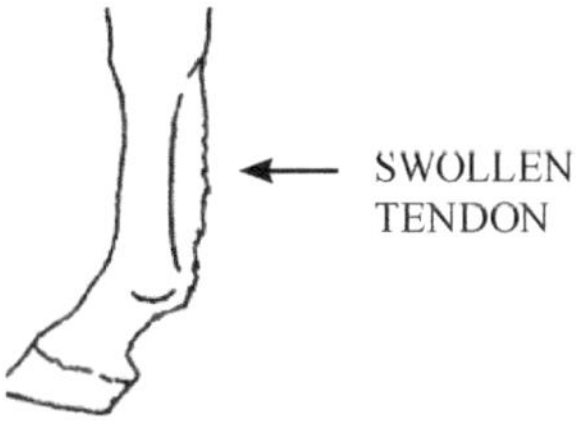

VETERINARY PROBLEMS

Virus	virus	***bee***rwus
Will it be alright?	estará bien?	ehstara been-ehn?
Wind sucker	tragador de aire	trahgadoor deh ***ah***-ee-reh
Windgalls	vejigas	beh-***hee***gas
Wormer	desparasitario	des-parahsit-ahryo
Wound powders	polvo para heridas	pohlbo parah eh***ree***dahs
Wound / injury	herida/lastimadura	eh***ree***dah / last-eemaduhra
Wounds	heridas	eh***ree***dahs
Xray	rayos x	rashos ekys

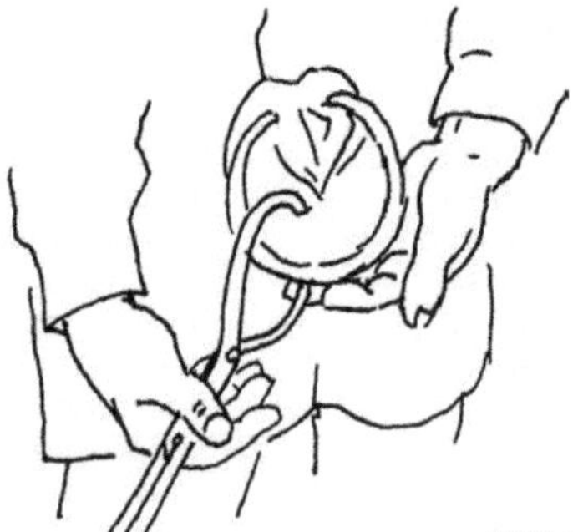

USE OF HOOF TESTER

8 | ORGANS and MUSCLES

Belly	vientre	bee-***ehn***treh
Belly: well proportioned	vientre: bien proporcionado	bee-***ehn***treh: byehn propor -seeoh***na***do
Body	cuerpo	kwerpo
Eyes	ojos	ohos
Joint	articulación	arteekoo***la***hseeon
Ligaments	ligamentos	leega***mehn***tos
Muscle atrophy	atrofia muscular	ah-trofya mooskoo***lahr***
Muscle strain	desgarro muscular	des-***ga***hrro mooskoo***lahr***
Muscles	músculos	***moos***koo-los
Organs	órganos	***oor***ga-nos
Pulled muscle	tirón muscular	tee***rohn*** mooskoo***lahr***
Swollen tendons	tendones inflamados	tehn-***don***-s eenflah-***ma***dos
Suspensory ligament	ligamento suspensorio	leega***mehn***to soos-pen-***so***ryo
Tendon sheath	vaina de tendón	bva-ee-nah deh tehn-don
Tendons	tendones	tehn-***don***-s
Thigh	muslo	moos-lo
Tongue	lengua	lehngwa
Twisted gut	nudo intestinal	noodo eentesteenahl
Windgalls	vejigas	beh-***hee***gas

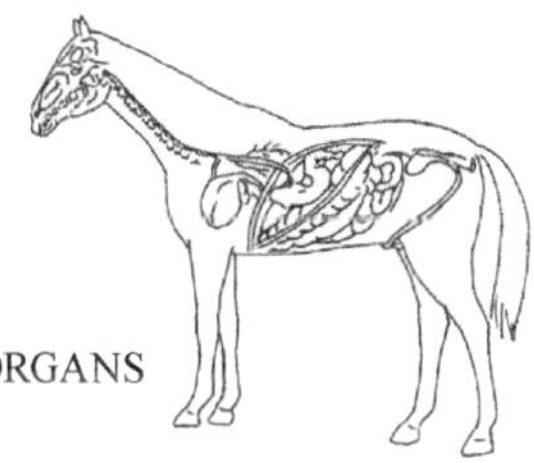

ORGANS

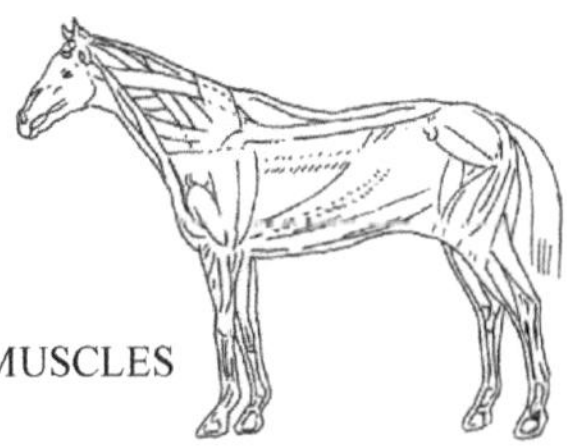

MUSCLES

9 | SKELETON

Back	lomo / espalda	lowmo / s-paldah
Back pain	dolor en la espalda	do***lohr*** n lah s-paldah
Bone spavin	esparaván	s-pahravan
Bones	huesos	wesos
Cannon bone	caña	kahnya
Caudal vertebrae	vértebras caudales	vehrtehbras kaudahl-es
Central pair of incisors	incisivos centrales	eensee-seebvos
Cervical vertebrae	vértebras cervicales	vehrtehbras cer-beekahl-es
Changing the teeth	cambio de dientes (dentición)	***kah***mbeeo deh dee-ehntehs
Coronet	corona	korona
Dock	rabo	rabo
Dorsal vertebrae	vértebras dorsales	vehr - teh - brass door***sah***les
Shoulder	hombro	ohmvro
Fetlock	nudos	noudos
Flanks/ Ribcage	costillares	kostee-***scha***-rres
Foot	pie	pee-eh
Fore / front legs	manos	manos
Forehead	frente	frehnteh
Frog	ranilla	rah***nee***scha
Head	cabeza	kabehsa

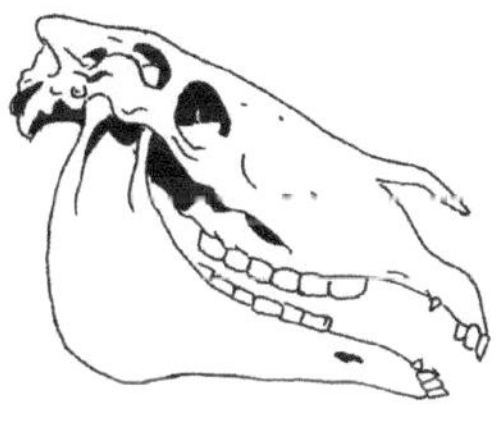
JAW

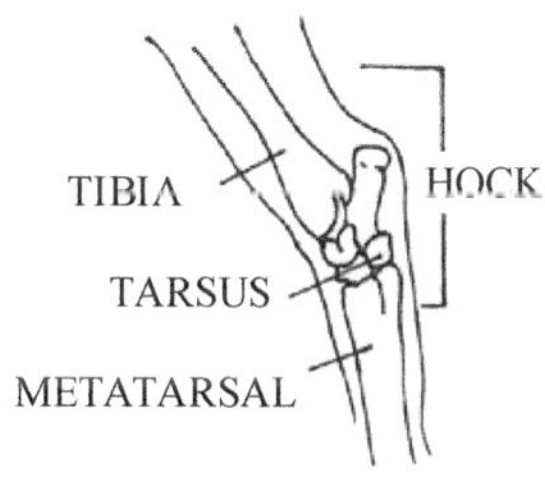

SKELETON

Hind legs	patas traseras	patas trah-cerahs
Hip	cadera	kah-dehra
Hock	corvejon	kohr-bvehon
Hoof	vaso	vahso
Incisor	incisivo	eensee-seebvo
Jaw	mandíbula	man***dee***boola
Joint	articulación	arteecoo***la***hsyon
Knee	rodilla	ro***dee***scha
Limbs	miembros	mee-ehmbro
Long neck	cogote largo	kogoteh lahrgo
Lower jaw	quijada	kee-hada
Lumbar vertebrae	vértebras lumbares	vehrtehbras lowm-***bahr***-es
Milk tooth	dientes de leche	dee-ehntehs deh lettcheh
Molar tooth	muela	mwela
Mouth	boca	boka
Navicular disease	enfermedad navicular	pro-bvlehma navee-koo***lahr***
Neck	cogote	kogoteh
Nose	hocico	oseeko
Nostrils	ollares	oh***sha***hrehs
Pastern	cuartilla	kwahr***tee***schas
Pelvis	pelvis	pehl-bees
Quarters	talones	tahl-on-es
Rasp [teeth] (to)	limar	lee***mahr***
Ribcage	pecho	petcho
Ribs	costillas	kos***tee***shas
Sacrum vertebrae	vértebras sacras	vehr-teh-bras sakras

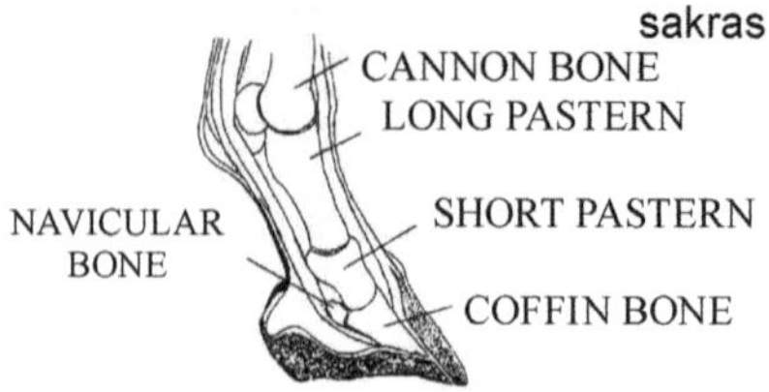

Shoe	herradura	eh-rra***doo***-ra
Shoulder blade	omóplato	o***mo***hplahto
Skeleton	esqueleto	s-keleto
Skull	cráneo	krah-neo
Splint	sobrehueso	sobrehgweso
Tail	cola	kola
Teeth	dientes	dee-ehntes
Thigh	muslo	moos-lo
To shoe a horse	herrar el caballo	ehrrahr l kabasho
Trim	desvasar	des-bva-sahr
Tushes	colmillos	kohl-***mee***schos
Upper-arm	brazo	brahso
Wall of the hoof	pared del vaso	pahrehd del vahso
Withers	cruz	krooz
Withers: high / wide	cruz: alta / ancha	krooz: alta / antcha

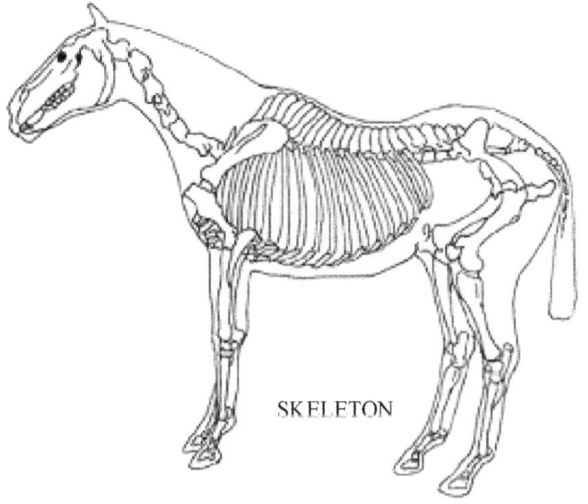

SKELETON

10 | CONFORMATION & TEMPERAMENT

Abortion	aborto	ahbvourto
Aggressive	agresivo	ahgrehseebo
Artificial insemination	inseminación artificial	een-sehmeenah-***syon*** artee-fee-seeahl
At withers	a la cruz	ah la krooz
Bad	mal	mahl
Bad traveller	viaja mal	vee-aha mal
Balance	balance	bah***lan***seh
Behaviour	comportamiento	komportahmyento
Behavioural problems	problemas de comportamiento	provlehmas deh komportahmyento
Belly	vientre	bee-ehntreh
Breast: wide, deep	pecho: amplio, profundo	pehtcho ampleeo, profoondo
Breeder	criador	kreeadoor
Breeding	crianza	kree***an***sah
Breeding horse	caballo de cría	kabasho deh kreea
Breeding selection	selección	sehlek***seeon***
Broken	domado	dohmado
Brood mare	yegua madre	shegwa madreh
Buck (to)	corcovear	korko-vee-ar
Buyer	comprador	kompradoor
Buying	comprando	komprando
Canter (to)	galopar	galoopahr

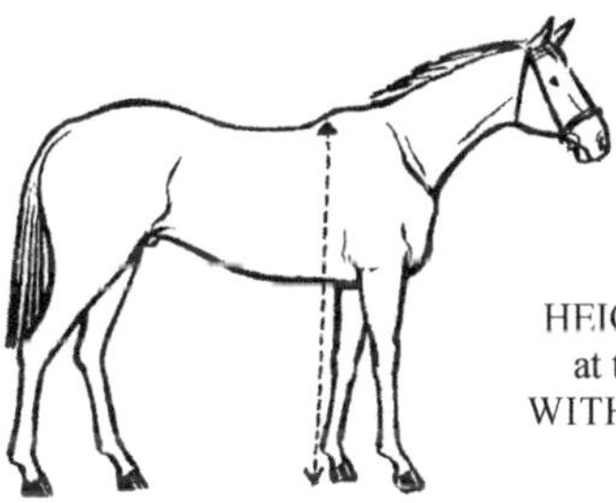

HEIGHT
at the
WITHERS

CONFORMATION & TEMPERAMENT

Cart horse	caballo de tiro	kabasho deh teero
Change legs (to)	cambiar de manos	kambeear deh mahnos
Character	carácter	kah-***ra***kter
Chest : broad	pecho: ancho	pehtcho antcho
Cold back	lomo duro	lomo dooh-ro
Collect (to)	reunir	reh-oo-neer
Colt	potro	pohtro
Compact	compacta	kompakta
Condition	condición	kon-dee***syon***
Conformation	conformación	konfor-mah-***syon***
Constitution	constitución	konsteetoo***seeon***
Correct horse	caballo correcto	kabasho ko***rr***ekto
Crib / biter	mordedor	mord-ehdoor
Dam	madre	madreh
Dead in the mouth	boca dura	boka doo-rah
Defects	defectos	dehfektos
Depth of girth	profundidad de pecho	profoundeedahd deh pehtcho
Dismount (to)	desmontar	dehs-mohn-***tahr***
Donkey	burro	***boo***-rro
Dry mouth	boca seca	boka sehka
Embryo transplant	transplante embrionario	transplanteh embreeoh***na***reeo
Empty mare	yegua vacia	shegwa vah***see***ah
Entire	caballo entero	kabasho entehro
Excellent	excelente	exellenteh
Expression	expresión	eksprehseeon
Fat	gordo	gourdo

Female	hembra	embra
Filly (maiden)	potranca	poutranka
Foal	potrillo	poh***tree***sho
Foal (to)	parir	pahreer
Foaling	pariendo	pahree-ehndo
Foot	pie	pee-eh
Geld (to)	castrar	kastrar
Gelding	caballo castrado	kabasho kastrado
General appearance	presencia general	preh***sen***seea
Give the reins	dar las riendas	dar las ree-ehndas
Good mouth	buena boca	bwena boka
Hack	caballo de montar	kabasho deh montahr
Half bred	cruza	kroosa
Heavy hands	manos pesadas	mahnos peh-***sa***das
Heel down	talon abajo	talohn ah-baho
Height (at withers)	alzada (en la cruz)	alsah-da (en la kroos)
Herd	manada	mahnada
Hold the reins	tener las riendas	ten-nehr las ree-ehndas
Horse	caballo	kabasho
Horse action	acción del caballo	akseeon dehl kabasho
Impulsion	impulsión	eempool***seeon***
Instructor	instructor	eens-trook-tohr

HORSE BALANCE
VERTICAL BALANCE (A=B=C=D)
HORIZONTAL BALANCE (E = F)

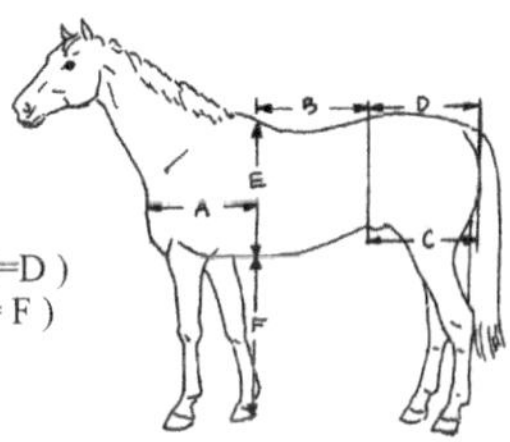

Iron brand	marca de hierro	mahrka deh yairro
Left handed	zurdo	szoo-rdo
Leg	pierna	pee-ehrna
Light canter	galope liviano	gah***lo***-peh lee-bee bahno
Long horse	caballo largo	kabasho largo
Loser	perdedor	pehr-deh-dor
Low	bajo	baho
Male	macho	matcho
Mane	clines	kleen-es
Mare	yegua	shegwa
Markings	marcas de pelaje	mahrkas deh peh***la***heh
Mating service	el servicio	el sehr-beeseeo
Mount	montar	mohn-tahr
Mouth	boca	boka
Narrow	angosto	anghosto
Normal respiration	respiración normal	respee-rah***seeon*** normahl
Origin	origen	oree-hen
Pain	dolor	dohl***ohr***
Parasites	parásitos	***para***hseetos
Passports	pasaportes	pahsaportehs
Pedigree	pedigree	peh-deegree
Polo pony	caballo de polo	kabasho deh polo
Position	posición	poh-see-***seeon***
Pregnant	preñada	prehnyada
Pull the reins	desbocarse	dess-bo-karseh

HIGH WITHERS

Race horse	caballo de carrera	kabasho deh kahrrera
Rearing	pararse de manos	pararseh deh mah-nos
Rein back (to)	recular	rekoo-lahr
Restricted movement	movimientos restringidos	mobeemyentos restreen-he-dos
Ribs	costillas	kos***tee***shas
Riding	equitación	aykeetah***seeon***
Riding lesson	lección de equitación	leksyon deh aykeetah***seeon***
Rig	pajero (el entero que se masturba)	pah-***he***ro
Roaring	roncador	ronkadoor
Served mare	yegua servida	shegwa sehrbeeda
Sex	sexo	sekso
Shorten the reins (to)	acortar las riendas	akortahr las ree-ehndas
Sire	padre	padre
Soft mouth	boca blanda	boka blanda
Stallion	semental	sehmentahl
Stubborn (to be)	empacarse	empakarseh
Stud book	stud book	stud book
Tall horse	caballo alto	kabasho altto
Teaser	celo	sehlo
Temperament	temperamento	tempehramento
The mare in foal	la yegua preñada	lah shegwa prehnyada
Thin	flaco	flako
Thoroughbred	pura sangre	pou-ra sangreh

CONFORMATION & TEMPERAMENT

Throw the rider (to)	tirar al jinete	teerahr al hee***ne***teh
Tongue over the bit	pasa la lengua	pah-sa la lehngwa
Tripping	tropezarse	tropesarseh
Trot (to)	trotar	trotahr
Type	tipo	tea-po
Unbroken	potro	pohtro
Unfit	desentrenado	des-entrehnado
Unpleasant	desagradable	des-ahgradah-bleh
Very good	muy bien	moo-ee bvee-ehn
Vices	vicios	***bee***-syos
Walk (to)	caminar	kahmeenar
Weaning the foal	el destete	ehl desteteh
Whistling	silbido	seelbeedo
Wide	ancha	antcha
Wind sucker	tragador de aire	trahgadoor deh ah-ee-reh
Wrong impresión	mala impresión	mala eemprehseeon
Yearling	potro de un año	poh***tree***sho

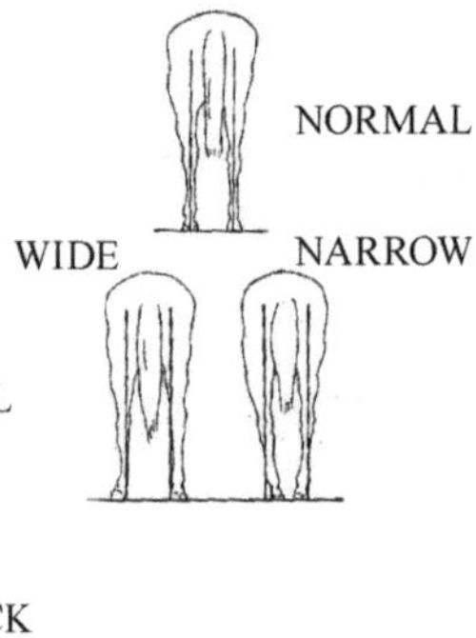

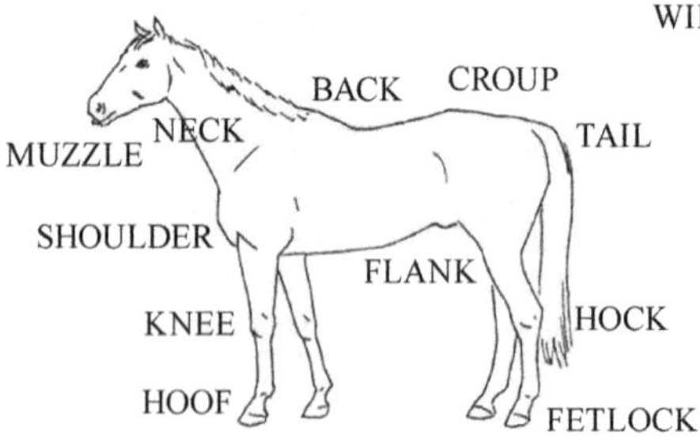

11 | COLORS and MARKINGS

Bay	zaina	tza-eenah
Black	negro	nehgro
Blaze	cordón corrido	kordohn ko***rree***do
Body	cuerpo	kwerpo
Brown	castaño oscuro	kastahnyo ooskooro
Chestnut	alazán	alah-san
Clipped mane	crin tuzada	kreen two-sahda
Clip (to)	tuzar	too-sahr
Coat	pelo	peh-lo
Colours	colores	kolohres
Coronet	corona	korona
Croup	anca	ahnka
Dock	rabo	rabo
Dorsal stripe	raya de gateado	rascha dehl lowmo (gat-eh-ahdo)
Dun	bayo	basho
Golden-chestnut	doradilla	dora-***dee***sha
Iron brand	marca de hierro	mahrka deh yairro
Light bay	zaina colorada	***tza***-eenah kohlorada
Mane	clines	kleen-es
Markings	marcas de pelaje	mahrkas deh pehlaheh
Piebald	tobiano negro	toh-beeahno neegro
Roan	rosillo	rosee-sscho

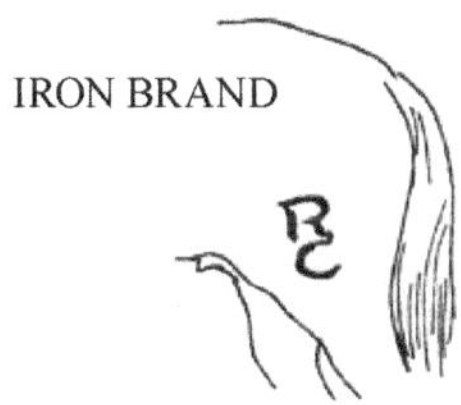

COLORS and MARKINGS

Skewbald	tobiano	toh-be**ea**hno
Snip	lunar entre ollares	loonahr en-treh o-scharehs
Star	estrella	estrescha
Stripe	raya	rascha
Summer coat	pelo de verano	pehlo deh veh-rahno
White (fore legs)	manos blancas	mahnos blahnkas
White heel	nudo blanco	noudo blahnko
White back / hinds legs	patas blancas	pahtas blahnkas
White on the coronet	corona blanca	korona blahnka
Winter coat	pelo de invierno	pehlo deh een-bvee-ehrno

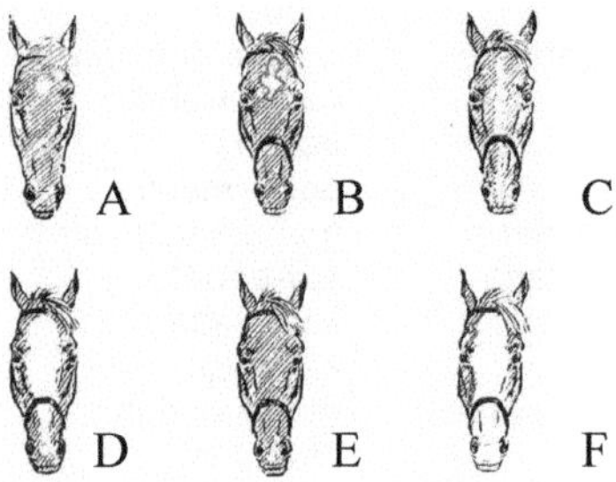

A- small star , B- star , C- stripe
D- blaze , E- snip , F- white face

WINTER CLIP

LEG MARKINGS

12 | FORAGE and MAINTENANCE

Alfalfa	alfalfa	alfalfa
Bale	fardo	***fa***hr-do
Barley	cebada	seh-va-dah
Bran	afrecho	ahfreh-tcho
Bucket	balde	bahldeh
Carrots	zanahorias	thana-orya
Cereal	cereal	sehreh-al
Chaff	paja picada	paha pee***ka***da
Clover	trebol	***tre***h-bohl
Corn	maíz	ma-ees
Corn oil	Aceite de maíz	ahsei-teh deh maees
Crushed/rolled/ oats	avena aplastada	ahbvenna ahplastada
Energy	energía	ener-***he***-ah
Feed	alimento	ah-leemento
Feeding	alimentando	ah-leementan-do
Field	campo	kahmpo
First cut	primer corte	pree-mehr kohr-teh
Forage	forraje	fore-ah-heh
Grass	pasto	pasto
Hard feed	balanceado	balan-zeado
Hay	fardo	fahr-do
Hay net	red	red
Hay rack	pastera	pastehra
Linseed oil	aceite de lino	ahsei-teh deh leeno

OAT

FORAGE and MAINTENANCE

Feed (to)	dar de comer	dahr deh ko-mehr
Feed bin	deposito de comida	deh***po***-seeto deh ko-meedah
Graze (to)	pastar	past-ar
Molasses	melaza	me***la***sah
Nutrition	nutrición	noo-tree-***syon***
Oat bin	depósito de avena	deh***po***-seeto deh ahbvenna
Oats	avena	ahbvenna
Pasture	pradera	prah-dehra
Pasture management	manejo de la pastura	mahneho deh la pas-too-rah
Ragwort (weed)	ragwort	ragwort
Ration	ración	rah-***seeon***
Rye	centeno	zen-tehno
Salt lick	sal	sal
Second cut	segundo corte	seh-goundo korteh
Soak hay	pasto mojado	pahsto moh-hado
Soya oil	aceite de soja	ahsei-teh deh zoha
Straw	paja	***pah***-ha
Water (to)	dar agua	dahr ahgwa
Weed	maleza	ma-***leh***-sa
Wheat	trigo	tree-go
Wheat straw	paja de trigo	pah-ha deh tree-go
Shade	sombra	***soh***mbrah

MANGER

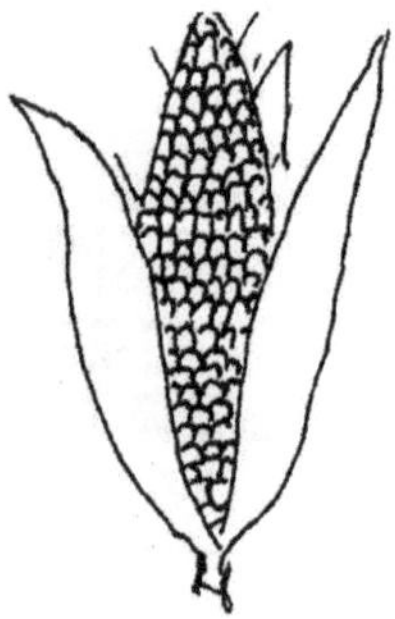

CORN

13 | EVERYDAY PHRASES

Nine ways to say *"HOW ARE YOU"*

How do you do? (very formal)	cómo esta usted?	***ko***-mo stah oostehd?
How are you doing?	cómo le va?	***ko***-moh leh vah?
How are things going?	cómo van las cosas?	***ko***-mo vahn lahs ko-sahs?
How are you? (formal)	cómo está usted?	***ko***-mo stah oostehd?
How are you? (informal)	cómo estas?	***ko***-mo stahs?
How are things?	qué tal?	***keh*** tahl?
What's up?	qué pasa?	***keh*** pahsa?
Nice to meet you	mucho gusto	mootcho goosto
Glad to meet you. (Very polite)	encantado de conocerlo	enkahntado deh konoh-serlo

ANSWER

So so	más o menos	mahs o meh-nohs
Very good	muy bien	moo-ee bvee-ehn
Fine, thanks	bien, gracias	bee-ehn, grass-seeahs

A few ways to say ***"NO"***

Not now, thanks	ahora no, gracias	ah-ohrah no, ***gra***ss-seeas
Not interested, thanks	no me interesa, gracias	no meh eentehrehsah, ***gra***ss-seeas
I don't like it	no me gusta	no meh goos-tah
I don't know	no se	no seh
Please, don't disturb me	no me moleste, por favor	no meh mohlehsteh, pohr fah-bvohr
No, thank you	no, gracias	no, ***gra***ss-seeas
No	no	no

ASKING QUESTIONS

Who?	quién?	kee-n?
What?	qué?	keh?
Where?	dónde?	***dohn***-deh?
When?	cuándo?	***kwa***ndo?
Why?	porqué?	pohr-***keh***?
How?	cómo?	***koh***-moh?
How much?	cuánto?	***kwa***hnto?
Which?	cuál?	kwahl?
What did you say?	qué dijo?	keh ***dee***-ho?

A few ways to be *POLITE AND MAKE FRIENDS*

Your name is...	te llamas...	teh shamahs...
Coffee at my house?	café en mi casa?	kahfeh en mee ***kah***sa?
In about ten minutes	en diez minutos	en dee-s meenotoos
At what time...?	a qué hora...?	ah keh ***oh***ra?
Can I...?	podría...?	pohdreea?
Cheers!	salud!	sah***loo*** !
Could you repeat that?	repite eso	re-***pe***te-eh esso?
Could you write it down?	puedes escribirlo?	pwedehs eskreebeerlo?
Do you do...?	hace usted...?	a-seh oostehd..?
Do you have a mobile, please?	tiene un movil, por favor?	tee-eh-nes oon mobveal, pohr fahbvohr?
Do you speak english?	hablas inglés?	ah-blah een-glehs?
Do you understand?	comprende?	com-prehnde?
Hello	hola	ola
I will send you a text	te mando un texto	teh mahndo oon texto
Well done	bien hecho	bee-ehn etcho
What is your address?	cuál es tu dirección?	kwahl es too deerek-***seeon***?
Where are the...?	dónde estan...?	***dohn-***deh es-tan..?
Where are you now?	dónde estas ahora?	***dohn***-deh ehstass ah-ora?
Where do you live?	dónde vives?	***dohn***-deh bee-ves
Where is it?	dónde está...?	***dohn***-deh stah ...?
Tomorrow night	mañana a la noche	mahnyana a lah notcheh

Sorry	disculpa	dees-k***ool***-pah
May I?	puedo?	p***weh***-do?
My address is...	mi dirección es..	me deerek-***seeon*** ehs....
My name is...	me llamo...	meh shamo.....
My telephone number is...	mi telefono es...	me te***leh***-fono-ehs..
Nice to meet you	mucho gusto	mootcho goosto
Ok	ok	ok
Please	por favor	pohr fah-bvohr
I don't speak spanish	no hablo español	no ah-blo espahneeohl
I don't understand	no entiendo	no en-tee-ehndo
I'm sorry	lo siento	lo see-***eh***nto
I'd like a...	quisiera un...	kees-sierra oon...
I'm leaving tomorrow	me voy mañana	meh boi mahnyana
Mr.	señor	sehneeor
Miss	señorita	sehneeo-rita
Mrs	señora	sehneeo-ra

FEW WAYS TO BE *"GRATEFUL"*

Yes	sí	see
Thank you very much	muchas gracias	mootchahs grass-seeahs
Thanks / thank you	gracias	grass-seeahs
Don't mention it	no hay de qué	no I deh keh
Excuse me	perdone	pehr-dohne
Fine thanks	bien, gracias	bee-ehn, grassseeahs
Glad to meet you	encantado de conocerlo	enkahntado deh konoh-serlo
Good bye / see you	hasta luego / Chau!	ahsta lwego / tchaouw
Good evening	buenas tardes	bwenas tar-dehs
Good morning	buen día	bwen deea
Good night	buenas noches	bwenas notches

COMPARATIVES

Large	grande	grahn-de
Larger	más grande	mahs grahn-de
Largest	el más grande	ehl mahs grahn-de
Small	pequeño	peh-kehneeo
Smaller	más pequeño	mahs peh-kehneeo
Smallest	el más pequeño	ehl mahs peh-kehneeo
Good	bueno	bweno
Better	mejor	meh-hor
Best	el mejor	ehl meh-hor
Exceptionally good	buenísimo	bwe***nee***-see-mo
Bad	malo	mahlo
Really bad	pésimo	***peh***-see-mo
Worst	peor	***peh***-ohr
Exceptionally bad	malísimo	mahl-ee-see-moh

~A buen entendedor, pocas palabras
(ah bwen ehn-tehn-deh-dohr, poh-kahs pah-lahvrahs)
~To the one who understands, few words.~

~Más vale pájaro en mano, que 100 volando
(mahs bvahle pah-hah-roh ehn mahno, keh 100 bvoh-lahndoh)
A bird in hand worth more than 100 flying

~Un error grande como una casa
(oon eh-rrohr grahn-deh koh-moh oo-nah kah-sah)
A mistake the size of a house~

~Pasó sin pena ni gloria
(pah-so seen pehnah nee gloh-ree-ah)
The event pass without pulling you down or lifting you up. Making no difference to you~

14 | USEFUL PHRASES

DRINKING, MEALS AND BEVERAGES

BBQ	asado	ah-sahdo
Beef	carne	karneh
Beer	cerveza	sir-bvesa
Chicken	pollo	po-sho
Coffee	café	kah-feh
Coffee w/ milk (white coffee)	café con leche	kah-feh kon letcheh
Creme caramel w/ dulce de leche	flan con dulce de leche	phlan kon doolse deh letcheh
Desert	postre	pohst-treh
Dinner	cena	sehna
Dulce de leche (Arg. Toffee spread)	dulce de leche	doolse deh letcheh
Empanada (Arg. Pastie)	empanada	empanahda
Fork	tenedor	teneh-door
Grill / BBQ	parilla	pahreesha
Knife	cuchillo	koochee-sho
Lamb	cordero	kord-ero
Lunch	almuerzo	al-moo-ehrso
Mate pot	mate	matteh

LAMB

ARG . KNIFE

EMPANADAS

CHICKEN

Mate leaf	yerba mate	sherbva matteh
Mate straw	bombilla	bom***bee***-sha
Mate with sugar	mate dulce	matteh doolseh
Pasta	Pasta	pasta
Pattiserie	factura	fak-***too***rah
Sheep	oveja	oh**ve**ha
Spoon	cuchara	kootchara
Steak	bife	vee-fe
Sugar	azúcar	ah-***soo***kar
Tea	té	teh
Torta frita	torta frita	tor-tah ***free***-tah
Wine	vino	bvee-no

TIME

Time	hora	ora
What time is it?	qué hora es?	keh ohra ess?
One o'clock	una en punto	oona n poo-nto
Ten past one	una y diez	oona ee dee-ehs
Quarter past one	una y cuarto	oona ee kwa-rrto
Twenty to two	dos menos veinte	doss mehnos bveh-ee-nteh
13:00	las trece horas / la una	lass treh-seh orass / lah oona
16:30	las diez y seis y treinta	lass dee-ehs ee sayss ee traynta
Noon	mediodía	meh-deeo dee-a
Midnight	medianoche	meh-deea notch-eh

COLLOQUIAL TERMINOLOGY

Bastard	cabrón	ka-brohn
Christ! / Shit!	carajo ! / mierda!	kah-rah-ho / mee-ehr-da
Dickhead (wanker)	forro	pho-rroh
Fool	boludo	bvo-***loo***-do
Gay	maricón	mahry-koun
Go on then!	dale!	daleh!
Good	bien	bee-ehn
I feel like it	me da la gana	meh dah la gah-na
Idiot	idiota	eedio-tah
Lazy bastard !	vago!	bvah-go!!
Listen	oiga!	oyga!
No way!	ni modo!	nee modo!
Old git	viejo verde	bvee-eh-ho behrdeh
Pain in the balls	hincha pelotas	eentcha pelo-tahs
Pickpocket	carterista	kart-teh-***ree***sta
Pig	cerdo	sehrdo
Poser	chanta	tchan-tah
Stupid	estúpido	estoo-pee-do
Where in hell?	dónde carajo ...?	dondeh kah-rahho...?
Where the shit is it?	dónde mierda está?	dondeh mee-ehr-da stah?
You are kidding me!	me estas jodiendo!	meh stahs hodee-ehndo!
You bastard	bastardo	bast-ardou
You screwed it up	lo jodiste	low hodeesteh

ATTENTION !!!
WE RECCOMEND TO USE THEM WITH MODERATION !!!!

DAYS

Days	días	deeas
Monday	lunes	***loo***n-es
Tuesday	martes	martt-es
Wednesday	miércoles	mee-***ehr***-kol-es
Thursday	jueves	hoo-eb-ehs
Friday	viernes	bvee-er-nehs
Saturday	sábado	***sha***bva-do
Sunday	domingo	do***meen***go
On Saturday	el sábado	ehl shabva-do
This Saturday	este sábado	ehsteh ***sha***bva-do
Next Saturday	el próximo sábado	ehl proxee-moe ***sha***bva-do
Last Saturday	el último sábado	ehl ***ool***t-eemo ***sha***bva-do
Every Saturday	todos los sábados	tohdos lohs ***sha***bva-dos
Today	hoy	oi
Tomorrow	mañana	mahnyana
Yesterday	ayer	ah-sher
This week	esta semana	stah seh***mah***-nah
Last week	la última semana	lah ***ool***t-eemah seh***mah***-nah
Next week	la próxima semana	lah proxee-mah seh***mah***-nah
Every day	todos los días	tohdos lohs deeas
All day	todo el día	tohdo ehl deeah
Next day	el próximo día	ehl proxee-moe deea
Week	semana	seh***mah***-nah

MONTHS

Months	meses	meh-sehs
Jannuary	enero	ehn-ero
February	febrero	febreh-ro
March	marzo	mahr-so
April	abril	ahvreel
May	mayo	masho
June	junio	hoo-nee-o
July	julio	hool-ee-o
August	agosto	ah-gohsto
September	septiembre	septee-ehm-breh
October	octubre	oktoo-vreh
November	noviembre	nohbvee-ehmbreh
December	diciembre	dee-see-ehmbvreh
Summer	verano	veh-rahno
Winter	invierno	een-bvee-ehrno
Before summer	antes del verano	ahntehs dehl veh-rahno
During summer	durante el verano	duhran-teh ehl veh-rahno
After summer	después del verano	dehspooehs del veh-rahno

ORDINALS

1°	primero	pree-mehro
2°	segundo	segoon-do
3°	tercero	tehrr-sehro
4°	cuarto	kwa-rrto
5°	quinto	keento
6°	sexto	seksto

USEFUL PHRASES

NUMBERS

Numbers	Números	noomehros
0	cero	sehro
1	uno	uhno
2	dos	dos
3	tres	ttres
4	cuatro	***kwa***tro
5	cinco	***seen***-ko
6	seis	***say***-ees
7	siete	***see***-eteh
8	ocho	otcho
9	nueve	nweb***veh***
10	diez	dee-ehs
20	veinte	bay-n-teh
30	treinta	***treh***eenta
50	cincuenta	sinkwenta
100	cien	see-ehn
200	doscientos	dos see-ehntos
300	trescientos	tres see-ehn-tos
1000	mil	meal
5000	cinco mil	seen-ko-meal

MEASURES

Height	altura	al-tour-ah
Measuring stick	bastón de medida	vahst-on deh med-eedah
At the withers	a la cruz	a la krooz

1 yard	0,9144 meters
1 mile	1,609 km
1 Km	0,62 miles
1 hand	10 cms
1 inch	2,5 cms
1 foot	30 cms
1 pound	0,454 kgrs
1 kilo	2.2 pounds
1 stone	6,35 kgrs
212 fahrenheit	100 celcius
32 farhrenheit	0 celcius

COLORS

Colors	colores	koh***lo***rehs
Black	negro	nehgro
Blue	azul	ah***sool***
Brown	marrón	mahrrohn
Green	verde	***beh***rdeh
Red	rojo	rro-ho
Sky blue	celeste	seh***les***teh
Violeta	violeta	beeo-letah
White	blanco	blahnko
Yellow	amarillo	amah***ree***sho

ALPHABETICAL ORDER

Abcess in the hoof	abceso en el vaso	mach-oo-kon
Abort	abortar	ahbvourtahr
Abortion	aborto	ahbvourto
Accessories	accesorios	akseh-***soh*** reeos
Accidents	accidentes	aksee-dentehs
Accommodation	vivienda	veevee-ehnda
Aggressive	agresivo	ahgrehseebo
Aids	ayudas	ah-shoodas
air	en el aire	ehn el ah- ee-reh
Alfalfa	alfalfa	alfalfa
All day	todo el día	tohdo ehl deeah
Anaemia	anemia	ah-nehmeea
Anaesthesia	anestesia	ah-nes-***te*** hsya
Analgesic cream	analgésico	ahnal-***he*** hseeko
Antifungal	antihongos	anteeongos
Antiseptics	antisépticos	anteesepteekos
April	abril	ahvreel
Arena	arena	arena
Arg. Horseman	gaucho	***ga*** ou-tcho
Artificial insemination	inseminación artificial	een-sehmeenah-syon artee-fee-seeah
At withers	a la cruz	ah la krooz
August	agosto	ah-gohsto
Back	lomo / espalda	lowmo / s-paldah
Back !	back!	back!
Back pain	dolor en la espalda	do***lohr*** n lah s-paldah
Back support	riñonera	rinyon-era
Back! (shot)	back (tiro de)	back
Bad	mal	mahl
Bad traveller	viaja mal	vee-aha mahl
Balance	balance	bah/***an*** seh
Bale	fardo	***fa*** hr-do
Ball	bocha	***bo*** ht-cha
Ball shy	aparta de la bocha	ahpartah deh la botcha
Bandages	vendas	venda-s
Bandages	vendajes	ven***da***-hes
Barley	cebada	seh-va-dah
Barn sour	mañero	mah-nee-eroh
Barren mare	yegua vacia	shegwa vahseea
Barry gag	doble barra	dobleh bah-rrah
Bastard	cabrón	ka-brohn
Bay	zaina	tza-eenah
BBQ	asado	ah-sahdo
Bed	cama	***ka*** ma
Bee	abeja	ah***be*** ha
Beef	carne	karneh
Beer	cerveza	sir-bvesa
Beginners	debutantes	deh-boo-***tahn*** tehs
Behaviour	comportamiento	komportahmyento
Behavioural problems	problemas de comportamiento	problemhas deh komportahmyento
Behind	atrás	ah-trahs
Belly	vientre	bee-***ehn*** treh
Best	el mejor	ehl meh-hor
Best player	mejor jugador	meh-hor hoogadohr
Best pony	mejor caballo	meh-hor kabasho
Bet	apuesta	apoo-ehsta
Better	mejor	meh-hor

Bite	mordedura	mor-deh-duhra
Bitting	mordedor	mord-ehdoor
Black	negro	nehgro
Blade	hoja	oh-ha
Blaze	cordón corrido	kordohn ko***rree*** do
Bleed (to)	sangrar	sahn-grahr
Bleeding	sangrando	sahn-grahn-do
Blister	ampolla	ampo-sha
Blistering	cáustico	***cow*** -steeko
Blood	sangre	sahn-greh
Blue	azul	ah***sool***
Blue book	libro de reglas	leebro deh rehglass
Boards	tablas	tabl-ahss
Body	cuerpo	kwerpo
Bolting	desbocarse	dess-bo-karseh
Bone spavin	esparaván	s-pahravan
Bone spavin inflamation	garrón inflamado	gah-rrohn eenflahmado
Bones	huesos	wesos
Boot jack	sacabotas	saka bvo-tas
Boots	botas	bvo-tas
Box	caja	***ka*** h-ha
Bran	afrecho	ahfreh-tcho
Breast: wide, deep	pecho: amplio,profundo	pehtcho ampleeo,profoondo
Breeder	criador	kreeadoor
Breeding	crianza	kree***an*** sah
Breeding horse	caballo de cría	kabasho deh kreea
Breeding selection	selección	sehlek***seeon***
Bridle	cabezada	kah-bezada
Broken	roto	rroto
Broken up (horse)	domado	dohmado
Brood mare	yegua madre	shegwa madreh
Broom (yard / wide)	escobillón	esko-bvee-shoohnn
Browband	frentera	fren-tehra
Brown	marrón	mahrrohn
Bruise	moretón	morayton
Brush	cepillo	seh***pee*** -sho
Brush (to)	cepillar	seh***peeh -shar***
Buck (to)	corcovear	korko-vee-ar
Bucket	balde	bahldeh
Buffalo hide	cuero de búfalo	kwero deh boo-fah-lo
Burns	quemaduras	kehmaduhra
Bute (phenylbutazone)	bute	bute
Buyer	comprador	kompradoor
Buying	comprando	komprando
Cannon bone	caña	kahnya
Canter (to)	galopar	galoopahr
Canter / gallop	galope	gah***lo*** hpeh
Captain	capitán	kapitan
Car	auto	aouto
Carrots	zanahorias	thana-orya
Cart horse	caballo de tiro	kabasho deh teero
Cash	efectivo	efek***tee*** bo
Caudal vertebrae	vértebras caudales	vehrtehbras kaudahl-es
Central pair of incisors	incisivos centrales	eensee-seebvos
Centre !	centro !	zentro

Cereal	cereal	sehreh-al
Cervical vertebrae	vértebras cervicales	vehrtehbras cer-beekahl-es
Chaff	paja picada	paha pee***ka*** da
Change (to)	cambiar	kambeear
Change leg in the	cambia las manos	kambya las manos
Change legs (to)	cambiar de manos	kambeear deh mahnos
Change of direction	cambiar dirección	kambeear deerehkseeon
Changing the teeth	cambio de dientes (dentición)	***kah*** mbeeo deh dee-ehntehs
Chaps	chaparreras	tchapa-***rre*** hras
Character	carácter	kah-***ra*** kter
Chest	pecho	petcho
Chest : broad	pecho: ancho	pehtcho antcho
Chestnut	alazán	alah-san
Chicken	pollo	po-sho
Cholic	cólico	***koh*** l-leeko
Christ ! / Shit !	carajo ! / mierda!	kah-rah-ho / mee-ehr-da
Chukka	chuker	tcha-kehr
Clean	limpio	***lee*** mpeeo
Clip (to)	tuzar	two-sahr
Clipper	tuzadora	two-sah-door-ah
Close	cerca	sehrka
Clover	trébol	***tre*** h-bohl
Coach	D . T.	deh-teh / coach
Coat	pelo	peh-lo
Coffee	café	kah-feh
Coffee w/ milk (white coffee)	café con leche	kah-feh kon letcheh
Cold back	lomo duro	lomo dooh-ro
Collect up (to)	reunir	reh-oo-neer
Collecting	colectar	kohl-ektahr
Colors	colores	koh***lo*** rehs
Colt	potro	pohtro
Comb (to)	peinar	peh-ee-nahr
Come back!	volvé!	ball-beh !
Compact	compacta	kompakta
Condition	condición	kon-dee***syon***
Conformation	conformación	konfor-mah-***syon***
Constitution	constitución	konsteetoo***seeon***
Contagious disease	enfermedad contagiosa	ehnfermedad konta-heeosa
Contract for xxxx	contrato por xxxx	kontrahto pohr xxxx
Cool down (to)	enfriar	n-free-ahr
Corn	maíz	ma-ees
Corn (vet.)	cayo	kasho
Corn oil	aceite de maíz	ahsei-teh deh maees
Coronet	corona	korona
Coronet boots	protector de corona	protektohr deh korona
Correct horse	caballo correcto	kabasho ko***rre*** kto
Coscojero	coscojero	kosko-hero
Cotton-wool	algodón	algoodoon
Cough	tos	tos
Coughing	tosiendo	tosee-ehndo
Cracked heels	talones agrietados	tahlonehs agreeeh-f***a*** hdos
Cracked hoof	rajaduras en los vasos	rahadowra en los vahsos
Cream	crema	krema
Creme caramel w / dulce de leche	flan con dulce de leche	phlan kon doolse deh letcheh
Crib / biter	mordedor	mord-ehdoor

Crossing the line	cruzando la linea	kroo-sahndo la leeneea
Croup	anca	ahnka
Crushed / rolled / oats	avena aplastada	ahbvenna ahplastada
Cup	copa	koppa
Curbchain	cadena de freno	kadehna deh frenoh
Curry comb	rasqueta	ras***ke***htah
Cut	cortadura	korta-duhra
Dam	madre	madreh
Danger	peligro	peh-***lee***gro
Date of arrival	día de llegada	deea deh shegahdah
Date of departure	día de partida	deea deh pahr***tee***da
Day off	día libre	deea leebreh
Days	días	deeas
Dead in the mouth	boca dura	boka doo-rah
Debility	debilidad	dehbeeleedad
December	diciembre	dee-see-ehmbvreh
Defects	defectos	dehfektos
Depth of girth	profundidad de pecho	profoundeedahd deh pehtcho
Desert	postre	pohst-treh
Diarrhoea	diarrea	dee-ah***rrea***
Dickhead (wanker)	forro	pho-rroh
Dictionary	diccionario	deekseeo-***na***rio
Dinner	cena	sehna
Dirty player	jugador sucio	hoogah-door sooseeo
Diseases	enfermedades	ehnfermedah-des
Disinfect	desinfectar	des-eenfektahr
Dismount (to)	desmontar	dehs-mohn-tahr
Distortion	dislocar	*dees-lo-* ***kahr***
Dizzy	mareado	mareh-addo
Dock	rabo	rabo
Doesn't stop	no para	no pahra
Don't mention it	no hay de qué	no i deh keh
Donkey	burro	***boo***-rro
Door	puerta	pwehr-tah
Dorsal stripe	raya de gateado	rascha dehl lowmo (gat-eh-ahdo)
Dorsal vertebrae	vértebras dorsales	***vehr***-teh-brass door***sa***hlehs
Dressing	apósito	***apo***seeto
Drinking trough	bebedero	bveh-bveh-dehro
Drinking water	agua potable	ahgwa po***ta***hvleh
Driving licence	licencia de conducir	leeszen-seeah deh kondooseer
Drop noseband	cierra boca	sierra boka
Droppings	bosta	bohsta
Dry mouth	boca seca	boka sehka
Dulce de leche (Arg. Toffee spread)	dulce de leche	doolse deh letcheh
Dun	bayo	basho
Dung	bosta(!)	bohsta(!)
Earlier	más temprano	mas temp-prano
Early training	entrenamiento temprano	ehntreh-nameeento temprahno
Embryo transplant	transplante embrionario	transplanteh embreeohnareeo
Empanada (Arg. Pastie)	empanada	empanahda
Empty mare	yegua vacia	ehegwa vah***see-*** ah
Energy	energia	ehner-***he***-ah
Entire	caballo entero	kabasho entehro
Entry fee	costo matrícula	ma***tree***-kwla
Equine influenza	gripe equina	***gree***-peh

Every day	todos los días	tohdos lohs deeas
Examination	examinación	eksa-meenah***seeon***
Excellent	excelente	exellenteh
Exceptionally good	buenísimo	bwe***nee***-see-mo
Excuse me	perdone	pehr-dohne
Exercise (to lead)	varear	varayahr
Exercise more	ejercitar más	eh-heseetahr mas
Exercise track	pista de vareo	peesta deh vareh-o
Experienced	experimentado	ekspehreementado
Expression	expresión	eksprehseeon
Eyes	ojos	ohos
Faceguard	protector de cara	protekt***or*** deh kahra
Fairplay	juego limpio	hoo-ego ***lee*** mpeeo
Fall (a)	caída	ka-***ee*** dah
Fall (to)	caer	ka-ehr
Far	lejos	lehos
Farrier	herrero	eh-***rre*** hro
Farrier (To prick by)	pinchar	peen-tchar
Fast	rápido	***ra*** peedo
Fat	gordo	gourdo
February	febrero	febreh-ro
Feed	alimento	ah-leemento
Feed (to)	dar de comer	dahr deh ko-mehr
Feed bin	deposito de comida	deh***po***-seeto deh ko-meedah
Feeding	alimentando	ah-leement-ando
Female	hembra	embra
Fence	empalizada	empahlee-sahda
Fertilization	fertilización	fertee-leezsah***seeon***
Fetlock	nudos	noudos
Fever	fiebre	fee-eh-breh
Field	campo	kahmpo
Field / ground	cancha	kancha
Figure 8	8 (ocho)	otcho
Filly (maiden)	potranca	poutranka
Finadyne (funixin	finadine	fee-nahdin
Fine thanks	bien, gracias	bee-ehn, grassseeahs
First aid kit	botiquín	bvoteekeen
First cut	primer corte	pree-mehr kohr-teh
Fit	entrenado	entrehnado
Fixed game	partido arreglado	pahr***tee*** do ahrreglahdo
Flanks/ Ribcage	costillares	kostee-***sha***-rres
Flap	solapa	so***la*** pa
Flexion test	prueba de flexion	prwebah deh **flek*syon***
Fly	mosca	***mo*** hska
Fly repellent	repelente	reh-pelenteh
Foal	potrillo	pohtreesho
Foal (to)	parto	pahr-tto
Foaling	pariendo	pahree-ehndo
Foaling (adj.)	parto	pahr-tto
Fool	boludo	bvo-***loo-*** do
Foot	pie	pee-eh
Forage	forraje	fore-ah-heh
Fore / front legs	manos	manos
Forehead	frente	frehnteh

Fork	tenedor	teneh-door
Fork (pitch)	horquilla	orh***kee*** sha
Foul	foul	foul
Fracture	fractura	fraktwra
Free hit	tiro libre	teero ***lee*** -bvreh
Friday	viernes	bvee-er-nehs
Frog	ranilla	rah***nee*** scha
Front	frente	frehnteh
Game	juego	hoo-ego
Gate	tranquera	trahn-kera
Gay	maricón	mahry-koun
Geld (to)	castrar	kastrar
Gelding	caballo castrado	kabasho kastrado
General appearance	presencia general	preh***sen*** seea
Girlfriend	novia	no-beeah
Girth	cincha	***seen*** tcha
Girth sores	sobaqueada	zsoba-keh-ada
Give the reins	dar las riendas	dar las ree-ehndas
Gloves	guantes	gwantehs
Go back (to)	bajar	vah-har
Go on then!	dale!	daleh!
Go up (to)	subir	soobeer
Go!	anda !	ahn***da*** !
Goal post	arco	ahrko
Goggles	antiparras	antee-***pa*** rras
Golden-chestnut	doradilla	dora-***dee*** sha
Good	bueno	bweno
Good bye / see you	hasta luego / Chau !	ahsta lwego / tchaouw
Good evening	buenas tardes	bwenas tar-dehs
Good manners	buenos modales	bwenos modal-es
Good morning	buen día	bwen deea
Good mouth	buena boca	bwena boka
Good night	buenas noches	bwenas notches
Grab	agarrar	ah-gahr-rrar
Grass	pasto	pasto
Graze (to)	pastar	past-ar
Grease (oil) the hooves	engrasar los vasos	ehngra-sar louhs vahsos
Green	verde	***beh*** rdeh
Grill / BBQ	parilla	pahreesha
Groom	petisero	pety-***se*** hro
Grooming	cuidado del caballo	kweedado dehl kabasho
Hack	caballo de montar	kabasho deh montahr
Hackamore	jacamor	hackamore
Half bred	cruza	kroosa
Half chaps	polainas	paul-ah-eenas
Half chukka	medio chukker	meh-deeo tcha-kehr
Half seat	medio asiento	meh-deeo ah-see-ehnto
Hand clipper	tuzadora de mano	too-sahdohra deh mano
Handicap	handicap	handicap
Hard feed	balanceado	balan-zeado
Hard ground	piso duro	peeso doo-ro
Hard mouth	boca dura	boka doo-rah
Hay	fardo	fahr-do
Hay net	red	red
Hay rack	pastera	pastehra

Head	cabeza	kabehsa
Headcollar	bozal	bvo-sal
Healing	curando	kooh**ra** ndo
Heavy	pesado	peh-sahdo
Heavy hands	manos pesadas	mahnos peh-**sa** das
Heel down	talon abajo	talohn ah-baho
Height (at withers)	alzada (en la cruz)	alsah-da (en la kroos)
Herd	manada	mahnada
Here	acá	a-kah
Hind legs	patas traseras	patas trah-cerahs
Hip	cadera	kah-dehra
Hit (to)	pegar	peh-gar
Hit it!	pegale!	peh-gal-eh !
Hobbles	manea	mah-**neh** -ah
Hock	corvejón	kohr-bvehon
Hold the reins	tener las riendas	teh-ner las ree-ehndas
Hoof	vaso	vahso
Hoof grease	grasa de vasos	grahsah deh vahsos
Hoof Tester	pinzas de vasos	**peen** zsas deh vahsos
Hoof-pick	limpia vasos	limp-eea vahsos
Hook (to)	trabar el taco	trahbar l tahko
Hook it!	trabalo !	trahbalo !
Horse (pony)	caballo	kabasho
Horse action	acción del caballo	akseeon dehl kabasho
Horse fly	tábano	**tah** bano
Horse walker	caminador	kahmee-nador
Horseshoe nail	clavos de herradura	klahbvos deh eh-rra**doo** -rah
Hose	manguera	mang-era
Hose down the horse (to)	bañar el caballo	bahnyar l kabasho
Hose leg	manguerear	man-gheh-reh-r
How is?	cómo esta?	komo ehsta?
Hurts here	duele aqui	dweleh akee
I feel like it	me da la gana	meh dah la gah-na
Ice	hielo	ee-ehlo
Idiot	idiota	eedio-tah
Impulse	impulso	eem**pool** so
Impulsion	impulsión	eempool**seeon**
Incisor	incisivo	eensee-seebvo
Infection	Infección	eenfek**syon**
Infectious anaemia	anemia infecciosa	**ahne** meea
Inflammation	inflamación	eenflahmah**seeon**
Inflammation of a Joint/arthritis	inflamación de articulación	eenflahmah**seeon** deh arteekoolahseeon
Influenza - cold (flu)	gripe, enfriamiento	greepeh /ehn-freeahmiento
In-foal mare	yegua preñada	shegwa prehneeada
Injection	inyección	eenjeck**syon**
Injuries	heridas	ehreedas
Inside	adentro	ahdehntro
Instructor	instructor	eens-trook-tohr
Intramuscular	intramuscular	inntramooskoo-**lahr**
Intravenous	intravenosa	inntrahbvenosa
Iron brand	marca de hierro	mahrka deh yairro
Jannuary	enero	ehn-ero
Jaw	mandíbula	man**dee** boola
Joint	articulación	arteekoolahseeon
July	julio	hool-ee-o

June	junio	hoo-nee-o
Kick (to)	patear	pate-ar
Kidney	riñón	reenyon
Knee	rodilla	ro***dee*** scha
Knee pads	rodilleras	rodee-sherahs
Knife	cuchillo	koochee-sho
Lamb	cordero	kord-ero
Lame (to be)	cojear / aflojar	ko-heh-ahr / a-flo-har
Laminitis	laminitis	lah-mee-nee-tees
Land (to)	aterrizar	ah-teh-ree-tsar
Large	grande	grahn-de
Larger	más grande	mahs grahn-de
Largest	el más grande	ehl mahs grahn-de
Last week	la última semana	lah ***ool*** t-eemah seh***mah*** -nah
Later	más tarde	mas ***tar*** -deh
Lazy bastard !	vago!	bvah-goü
Lead rope	cabestro	ka***bes*** tro
Leading	de tiro	deh tee-ro
Lean on the bit	apoya en el freno	ahpo-sha en el freh-no
Learn to play polo	aprender a jugar al polo	ahprendehr a hoogahr al polo
Leave it!	dejala !	deh-hala!
Left handed	zurdo	szoo-rdo
Leg	pierna	pee-ehrna
Lice	piojo	peeo-ho
Lift the foot up	levantar la mano	leh-bvantahr lah mahno
Ligament (suspensory)	ligamento (suspensorio)	leegamehnto (soos-pen-soryo)
Ligaments	ligamentos	leega***mehn*** tos
Light	luz	loos
Light bay	zaina colorada	f***za*** -eenah kohlorada
Light canter	galope liviano	gah***lo*** -peh lee-bee-ahno
Limbs	miembros	mee-ehmbro
line out	salida afuera	sal-eedah ahfwerah
line of ball	lÍnea de la bocha	leenya deh la botcha
Linseed oil	aceite de lino	ahsei-teh deh leeno
Liquid paraffin	parafina líquida	parahfeenah ***lee*** keeda
Listen!	oiga!	oyga!
Listen to me	escúchame	es**koo**tchameh
Long horse	caballo largo	kabasho largo
Long neck	cogote largo	kogoteh lahrgo
Loosen the reins	dar las riendas	dahr las ree-ehndas
Lorry / truck/horsebox	camión	kahm***eeon***
Loser	perdedor	pehr-deh-dor
Low	bajo	baho
Lower jaw	quijada	kee-hada
Lumbar vertebrae	vértebras lumbares	vehrtehbras lowm-***bahr*** -es
Lunch	almuerzo	al-moo-ehrso
lunging	a la soga	ah la zohga
Lytes (electrolytes)	sales	sal-ess
Make a pony (to)	hacer un caballo	ahcehr oon kabasho
Male	macho	matcho
Mallet / stick	taco	tako
Management	dirección	deereck***seeon***
Mane	crines	kleen-es
Manger	comedero	koh-me***dero***
March	marzo	mahr-so

Mare	yegua	shegwa
Mare in foal	yegua preñada	shegwa prehnyada
Markings	marcas de pelaje	mahrkas deh pehlaheh
Married - single?	casado - soltero?	kahsado - sohl-tehro?
Martingale	bajador	baha-dor
Masseur / osteopath	masajista	mah-sa-h**ees** ta
Masssage	masaje	ma**ssa** heh
Match	partido	pahr**tee** do
Mate leaf	yerba mate	sherbva matteh
Mate pot	mate	matteh
Mate straw	bombilla	bom**bee**-sha
Mate with sugar	mate dulce	matteh doolseh
Mating service	el servicio	el sehr-beeseeo
May	mayo	masho
Me ! (to)	a mí !	ah mee!
Medicines	medicinas	mehdee**see** nas
Médium and high Goal	mediano y alto handicap	meh**dee** ano / ahlto handicap
Members	miembros	mee-embrross
Menage (Arena)	picadero	peak-ahdehro
Midnight	medianoche	meh-deea notch-eh
Milk tooth	dientes de leche	dee-ehntehs deh lettcheh
Mine!	mía !	meea !!!
Minutes	minutos	mee-nootos
Miss	señorita	sehneeo-rita
Molar tooth	muela	mwela
Molasses	melaza	me***la*** sah
Monday	lunes	***loo*** n-es
Money	plata	pla-tah
Months	meses	meh-sehs
Mount	montar	mohn-tahr
Mouth	boca	boka
Mouth piece	embocadura	embo-ka-doora
Movement	movimientos	mobeemyentos
Mr.	señor	sehneeor
Mrs	señora	sehneeo-ra
Muck out	hacer la cama	ah-sir lah kama
Mud fever	infección cutánea	eenfek***syon*** koof***ah*** nya
Muscle atrophy	atrofia muscular	ah-trofya mooskoo/***ahr***
Muscle strain	desgarro muscular	des-***ga*** hrro mooskoo***lahr***
Muscles	músculos	***moos*** koo-los
Muzzle	trompeta	trom-***pe*** tta
Nail	clavo	***klah*** *-bo*
Nail up (to)	clavar	klah-***bar***
Name	nombre	***noh*** mbreh
Narrow	angosto	anghosto
Navicular disease	enfermedad navicular	pro-bvlehma navee-koo***lahr***
Nearside forehand	revés	reh-bves
Neck	cogote	kogoteh
Neckshot (hit)	cogote	kogoteh
Next day	el próximo día	ehl proxee-moe deeah
Next week	la próxima semana	lah proxee-mah seh***mah***-nah
No way!	ni modo!	nee modo!
Noon	mediodía	meh-deeo dee-a
Normal breathing	respiración normal	res-pee-rah***seeon*** noormahl
Nose	hocico	oseeko

Nostrils	ollares	oh***sha*** hrehs
November	noviembre	nohbvee-ehmbreh
Nutrition	nutrición	noo-tree-***syon***
Oat bin	depósito de avena	deh***po*** -seeto deh ahbvenna
Oats	avena	ahbvenna
October	octubre	oktoo-vreh
Offside backhand	back	back
Offside forehand	por derecho	por dehretcho
Old git	viejo verde	bvee-eh-ho behrdeh
On the left leg	zurdo	szoo-rdo
Open !	abierto!	ahbee-ehrto !
Open wound	herida abierta	ehreedah ahbee-eh-rrta
Organs	órganos	***oo*** rga-nos
Origin	origen	oree-hen
Osteopath	masajista	mah-sa-h**ee** sta
Out	afuera	ah-fooehra
Out of bounds - off	fuera de cancha	fwera deh la kancha
Outdoor rug	manta de campo	manta deh kampo
Outdoor school	picadero	peekadayro
Over here	hacia aquí!	ah-**seea** ahkee !
Overreach boots /coronet boots	protector de corona	protektohr deh korona
Paddock	potrero	poht-rehro
Pain	dolor	doh***lohr***
Pain in the balls	hincha pelotas	eentcha pelo-tahs
Pain in the leg	dolor en la pierna	doh***lohr*** ehn la pee-ehrna
Panel (saddle)	bastos	baastos
Parasites / Worms	parásitos	pa***ra*** hseetos
Partition	partición	part-ee***syon***
Passports	pasaportes	pahsaportehs
Pasta	Pasta	pasta
Pastern	cuartilla	kwahrt**ee** schas
Pasture	pradera	prah-dehra
Pattiserie	factura	fak-***too*** rah
Pedigree	pedigree	peh-deegree
Pelham	pelam	peh-lam
Pelvis	pelvis	pehl-bees
Penalty	penal	pehnal
Penalty from the spot	penal del lugar	pehnal dehl lougahr
Pick out the hoof	limpiar los vasos	leempyar lohs vahsos
Pickpocket	carterista	kart-teh-***ree*** sta
Piebald	tobiano negro	toh-beeahno neegro
Pig	cerdo	sehrdo
Pinfiring	puntas de fuego	pwntas deh fwehgo
Pipe opener	dar aire	dar ah-ee-reh
Pitch fork	horquilla	or***kee*** sha
Plait tail (to)	trenzar cola	tren-zsar kola
Play it !	jugala!	hoogahlah!
Player	jugador	hoo-gah-door
Pneumonía	pulmonía	poolmo***nee*** ah
Polo field	cancha	kancha
Polo gag	levantador	leh-ban-tah-dor
Polo helmet	casco de polo	kasko deh polo
Polo pony	caballo de polo	kabasho deh polo
polo stud	taco	tako
Pommel	pomo	pomo

Ponylines	palenques	pahl-n-kes
Poser	chanta	tchan-tah
Position	posición	pohs-see-***seeon***
Poultice	compresa	kompressa
Practice	práctica	***pra*** kteeka
Pregnant	preñada	prehnyada
Preparation	preparación	preh-parah-seeon
proportioned	proporcionado	propor -seeoh***na*** do
Pull the reins	desbocarse	dess-bo-karseh
Pulled muscle	tirón muscular	*tee* ***rohn*** mooskoo-***lahr***
Pulse (bits)	pulso	poolso
Pulse rate (bit rate)	pulsación	poolsa-***syon***
Pus	pus	poos
Quarantine	cuarentena	kwaren***teh*** na
Quarters	talones	tahl-on-es
Race horse	caballo de carrera	kabasho deh kahrrera
Ragwort (weed)	ragwort	ragwort
Raining	lloviendo	shoo-bvee-ehndo
Raise the foot (to)	levantar la mano	lehbvantahr lah mano
Ramp	rampa	rampa
Rasp	escofina	esko-***fee***-nah
Rasp (to)	limar	leemahr
Ration	ración	rah-***seeon***
Raw hide	cuero crudo	kwero ***kroo*** do
Really bad	pésimo	***peh***-see-mo
Rear up	encabritarse	enka-bree-tahrseh
Rearing	pararse de manos	pararseh deh mah-nos
Recovery	recuperación	rehkoopeh-rah***seeon***
Red	rojo	rro-ho
Red worms	estrongilos	es***tron***-heelos
Referee	referí	reh-feh-ree
Rein back (to)	recular	rehkoo-lahr
Reins	riendas	ree-ehndas
Relaxed	relajado	rehla-hado
Remove the shoe	sacar herraduras	sah-kar ehrra-doorahs
Respiration	respiración	respeerah***seeon***
Rest period	período de descanso	peh-***ree***-oodo deh dehskanso
Restricted movement	movimientos restringidos	mobeemyentos restreen-he-dos
Ribcage	pecho	petcho
Ribs	costillas	kos***tee*** shas
Ride bareback (to)	montar en pelo	montahr en peh-lo
Ride him off!	sácalo!	sakahlo!
Ride off (to)	tomarlo	to-mahr- lo
Rider's Equipment	equipo	ehkeepo
Riding	cabalgar /equitación	kahbalgahr /aykeetahseeon
Riding lesson	lección de equitación	leksyon deh aykeetahseeon
Rig	pajero (el entero que se masturba)	pah-***he*** ro
Right of way	derecho de paso	deh-rehtcho deh pahso
Roan	rosillo	rosee-sscho
Roaring	roncador	ronkadoor
Room	cuarto	kwahr-to
Rug	manta	mahnta
Rules	reglas	rehglas

Running reins	riendillas	ree-ehndee-shas
Rye	centeno	zen-tehno
Sacrum vertebrae	vértebras sacras	vehr-teh-bras sakras
Saddle	montura	mohn***too*** rah
Saddle cloth	matra	matra
Saddle pad	goma espuma	goma espooma
Saddle tree	armazón	arma***thon***
salt lick	sal	sal
Satisfactory	satisfactorio	sateesfactoryo
Saturday	sábado	***sa*** hbva-do
School (to)	dar escuela	dar eskwehla
Scissors	tijeras	tee-***he*** ras
Score	gol	gol
Season (To be in)	celo	sehlo
Seat	asiento	ahsee ento
Second cut	segundo corte	seh-goundo korteh
September	septiembre	septee-ehm-breh
Served mare	yegua servida	shegwa sehrbeeda
Severe bit	freno severo	frehno seh-bero
Sex	sexo	sekso
Shade	sombra	***soh*** mbrah
Shaving	viruta	vee-roo-tah
Sheep	oveja	oh***ve*** ha
Shelter	cobertizo	kober***tee*** so
Shirt	remera	reh-mehras
Shoe	herradura	eh-rra***doo***-ra
Shoe a horse (to)	herrar el caballo	ehrrahr l kabasho
Shoeing	herrando	eh-***rrahn-*** do
Shooling in a circle	dar círculos	dar ***seer*** koolos
Shorten the reins	acortar las riendas	akortahr las ree-ehndas
Shoulder	hombro	ohmvro
Shoulder blade	omóplato	o***mo*** hplahto
Shovel	pala	pahla
Side	costado	cost-ahdo
Sire	padre	padre
Skeleton	esqueleto	s-keleto
Skewbald	tobiano	toh-be***ea*** hno
Skid boots	pichiqueras	peetchikeras
Skull	cráneo	krah-neo
Sky blue	celeste	seh***les*** teh
Slow	despacio	des-***pah*** seeo
Small	pequeño	peh-kehneeo
Smaller	más pequeño	mahs peh-kehneeo
Smallest	el más pequeño	ehl mahs peh-kehneeo
Snaffe/ gag	filete	feel-ehte
Snip	lunar entre ollares	loonahr en-treh o-scharehs
Soak hay	pasto mojado	pahsto moh-hado
Soap	jabón	ha-bohn
Soft ground	piso blando	peeso blando
Soft mouth	boca blanda	boka blanda
Sole	suela	swelah
Soya oil	aceite de soja	ahsei-teh deh zoha
Spasm	espasmo	s-pasm-o
Speak english? (Do you)	habla inglés?	ah-blah een-glehs?
Splint	sobrehueso	sobrehgwoso

Sponge	esponja	es***pohn***-ha
Spoon	cuchara	kootchara
Sprained tendons	tendones inflamados	tehn-***don***-s eenflah-mahdos
Spurs	espuelas	espwelas
Stable	box	box
Stable / yard	caballeriza	kah-bah-she***ree*** za
Stable bandage	venda de descanso	vehndah deh deskahnso
Stable-cloth	trapo	***tra*** hpo
Stallion	semental	sehmentahl
Star	estrella	estrescha
Start	comienzo	komee-enso
Steak	bife	vee-fe
Stick and ball (to)	taquear	ta-keh-ar
Sting	picadura	peekadoora
Stirrup leathers	estriberas	estree-bveras
Stirrup lenght	largo de estriberas	largo deh las estree-beras
Stirrups	estribos	estree-boos
Stomach	estómago	esto-mahgo
Stop well (to)	para bien	pah-rah bee-ehn
Stop!	frena !	frehna !
Strain	desgarro	desgahrro
Strangles	paperas	pah-peras
Straps	tiras	teeras
Straw	paja	***pah***-ha
Stretch the neck	estirar el cogote	estee-rahr el kogoteh
Stripe	raya	rascha
Stubborn (to be)	empacarse	empakarseh
Stud book	stud book	stud book
Stud fee	el costo de servicio	kohsto dell cerveeseeo
Stupid	estúpido	estoo-pee-do
Sugar	azúcar	ah-***soo*** kar
Summer	verano	veh-rahno
Summer coat	pelo de verano	pehlo deh veh-rahno
Summer rug	manta de verano	manta deh veh-rahno
Sunday	domingo	do***meen*** go
Surcingle	sobrecincha	sobray***see*** ntcha
Surgery	cirugía	seer-oouheea
Suspensory ligament	ligamento suspensorio	leega***mehn*** to soos-pen-soryo
Sweat (to)	sudar	soodahr
Sweat scraper	secador	sek-a- door
Swelling	inflamación	eenfamahsyon
Swollen tendons	tendones inflamados	tehn-***don***-es eenflah-mahdos
Syringe	jeringa	hereengah
Tack	equipo	eh***kee*** po
Tactics	tácticas	***tak*** teeekas
Tack room	monturero	montoo-***re*** hro
Tacking up	ensillando	ens-see-shando
Tail	cola	kola
Tail wrap/bandage	colera	kohl-ehra
Tail!	cola!	kola!
Take it! (ball)	tómala!	to-mah-la
Take the man	tomar al hombre	to-mahr al ohmbreh
Takes good care of	cuida muy bien	kweeda mwee beeehn
Tall horse	caballo alto	kabasho altto
Tape	cinta	seentah

Tapeworms	tenias	tehneeas
Tea	té	teh
Team	equipo	eh***kee*** po
Teaser	celo	sehlo
Teeth	dientes	dee-ehntes
Telephone	teléfono	te***leh*** -fono
Temperament	temperamento	tempehramento
Temperature	temperatura	temperah-toora
Tendon boots	tendoneras	tehn-don-ehras
Tendon sheath	vaina de tendón	bva-ee-nah deh tehn-don
Tendons	tendones	tehn-***don*** -s
Tetanus	tétano	tehtano
Thanks / thank you	gracias	grass-seeahs
There	allá	asha
Thermometer	termómetro	termohmetro
Thigh	muslo	moos-lo
Thin / skinny	flaco	flako
Thoroughbred	pura sangre	pou-ra sangreh
Thread worms	oxiuros	ohkseewroos
Throw in	salida	sah***lee*** da
Throw the rider (to)	tirar al jinete	teerahr al hee***ne*** teh
Thrush (in hoof)	hormiguero	or-mee-ggero
Thursday	jueves	hoo-eb-ehs
Tighten/ undo the ……..	ajusta/ afoja la ……..	ahoosta/ a-floha la ………
Time	hora	ora
Time out	tiempo fuera	tyempo foo-ehra
Today	hoy	oi
Tomorrow	mañana	mahnyana
Tongue	lengua	lehngwa
Tongue over the bit	pasa la lengua	pah-sa la lehngwa
Topical	superfcial	superfee***syal***
Torta frita	torta frita	tor-tah ***free*** -tah
Tournament	torneo	tor-neh-oh
Track	pista	***pee*** sta
Trailer	trailer	trah-eeler
Training	entrenamiento	ehn-treh-nameeento
Transport	transporte	trahns***por*** teh
Travel boots	botas de viaje	boht-ahs deh veeah-heh
Trim (hooves)	desvasar	des-bva-sahr
Trim hooves (to)	desvasar	des-bvah-sahr
Tripping	tropezarse	tropesarseh
Trophy	trofeo	tro-feh-o
Trot (to)	trotar	trotahr
Truck / lorry	camión	kah***meeon***
Tuesday	martes	martt-es
Turn it !	redondilla!	reh-dondeesha!
Turn out (to)	soltar en el corral	zoltahr en l korrahl
Turn!	dobla!	dohblah !
Turns badly	dobla mal	dohblah mal
Tushes	colmillos	kohl-***mee*** schos
Twisted gut	nudo intestinal	noodo eentesteenahl
Twitch	mordaza	mor***da*** zsa
Type	tipo	tea-po
Umpire	umpire	umpire
Umpire pony	caballo de referí	kabasho deh referi
Unbroken	potro	pohtro

Unfit	desentrenado	des-entrehnado
Unpleasant	desagradable	des-ahgradah-bleh
Untacking	desensillando	deh-zen-seeshando
Upper-arm	brazo	brahso
Vaccination	vacunación	bvakoonah***seeon***
Vaccine	vacuna	bva***koo*** na
Vaseline	vaselina	bvaseh-***lee*** na
Very bad player	choto	tchoto
Very good	muy bien	moo-ee bvee-ehn
Vet	veterinario	beh- teh-ree-***na*** ryo
Vices	vicios	***bee***-syos
Violeta	violeta	beeo-letah
Virus	virus	***bee*** rwus
Wage	salario	salah-reeo
Walk (to)	caminar	kahmeenar
Wall of the hoof	pared del vaso	pahrehd del vahso
Warm up	precalentar	preh-kalentar
Wash (to)	lavar	lavahr
Water	agua	agwa
Water (to)	dar agua	dahr ahgwa
Weaning the foal	el destete	ehl desteten
Wednesday	miércoles	mee-***ehr***-kol-es
Weed	maleza	ma-***leh***-sa
Week	semana	seh***mah***-nah
Week (this)	esta semana	stah seh***mah***-nah
Wheat	trigo	tree-go
Wheat straw	paja de trigo	pah-ha deh tree-go
Wheel-barrow	carretilla	kahrreteesha
Whip	fusta	foosta
Whistle	silbato	seal-bato
Whistling	silbido	seelbeedo
White	blanco	blahnko
White (fore legs)	manos blancas	mahnos blahnkas
White back / hinds legs	patas blancas	pahtas blahnkas
White heel	nudo blanco	noudo blahnko
White on the coronet	corona blanca	korona blahnka
Whites	blancos	blahnkos
Wide	ancha	antcha
Wind sucker	tragador de aire	trahgahdoor deh ***ah***-ee-reh
Windgalls	vejigas	beh-***hee*** gas
Wine	vino	bvee-no
Winner	ganador	gahnador
Winter	invierno	een-bvee-ehrno
Winter coat	pelo de invierno	pehlo deh een-bvee-ehrno
Wipe dry (to)	secar	sekahr
Withers	cruz	krooz
Withers: high / wide	cruz: alta / ancha	krooz: alta / antcha
Wooden horse	caballo de madera	kabasho deh mah***de*** hra
Work permit	permiso de trabajo	pehr***m-ee*** so deh trahba-ho
Wormer	desparasitario	des-parahsit-ahryo
Worst	peor	***peh***-ohr
Wound / injury	herida / lastimadura	eh***ree*** dah / last-eemaduhra
Wound powders	polvo para heridas	pohlbo parah eh***ree*** dahs
Wrist support	muñequera	moonyeh-kera
Wrong impression	mala impresión	mala eemprehseeon

Xray	rayos x	rashos ekys
Yards	yardas	tshardas
Yes	sí	see
Yearling	potro de un año	poht***ree*** sho
Yellow	amarillo	amah***ree*** sho
Yesterday	ayer	ah-sher
Your line!	tu línea!	too leeneea
Yours!	tuya!	tooscha !

* 9 7 8 1 7 8 0 3 5 4 2 1 7 *

SD - #0018 - 050826 - C0 - 180/130/5 - PB - 9781780354217 - Gloss Lamination